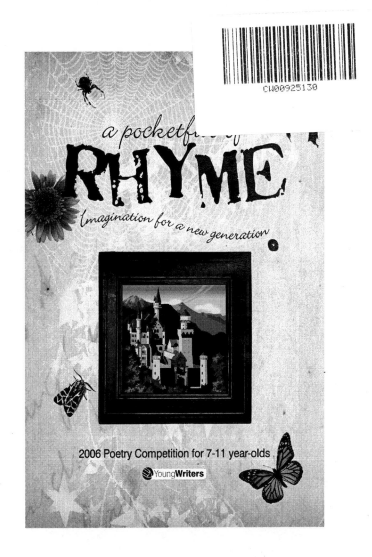

a pocketful of

RHYME

Imagination for a new generation

2006 Poetry Competition for 7-11 year-olds

YoungWriters

Southern Rhymes

Edited by Lynsey Hawkins

 Young**Writers**

First published in Great Britain in 2007 by:
Young Writers
Remus House
Coltsfoot Drive
Peterborough
PE2 9JX
Telephone: 01733 890066
Website: www.youngwriters.co.uk

SB ISBN 1 84602 720 9

Foreword

Young Writers was established in 1991 and has been passionately devoted to the promotion of reading and writing in children and young adults ever since. The quest continues today. Young Writers remains as committed to the nurturing of poetic and literary talent as ever.

This year's Young Writers competition has proven as vibrant and dynamic as ever and we are delighted to present a showcase of the best poetry from across the UK and in some cases overseas. Each poem has been selected from a wealth of *A Pocketful Of Rhyme* entries before ultimately being published in this, our fourteenth primary school poetry series.

Once again, we have been supremely impressed by the overall quality of the entries we have received. The imagination, energy and creativity which has gone into each young writer's entry made choosing the poems a challenging and often difficult but ultimately hugely rewarding task - the general high standard of the work submitted ensured this opportunity to bring their poetry to a larger appreciative audience.

We sincerely hope you are pleased with this final collection and that you will enjoy *A Pocketful Of Rhyme Southern Rhymes* for many years to come.

Contents

Oliver Joy (9)	17
William Lee (10)	18
Lilly Mann (8)	18
James Cockayne (9)	19
Alexander McGrigor (9)	19
Henry Marden (9)	20
Olivia 'Liv' Williams (8)	20
Lewis Marden (10)	21
Victoria Childs (10)	21
Holly Nicholls (10)	22
Georgina Lewis (10)	23
Thomas Shakespeare (10)	24
Louis Ambrose (11)	25
Harry Vokins (11)	26
Marsha Allan-Burns (9)	26
Conor Bevens (10)	27
Grace Taylor (9)	27
Chloe Larby (8)	28
Arabella Watkiss (10)	29
Mattea Pauc (8)	30
Frazer Poulter (8)	30
Anya Jackson (9)	31
Valentina Sassow (8)	31
Katie Newsom (9)	32
Posy Hewitt (9)	33
Keir Amyes-Headley (9)	34
Felix Ambrose (9)	34
James Wood (9)	35
Tim Morgan (9)	35
Eliza Cudmore (8)	36
Hugo Walters (10)	37
Joseph Holland (9)	38
Theo Seely (8)	38
Jasper Slawson (9)	39

Kempshott Junior School, Basingstoke

Lucy Edwards (10)	39
Liam Askew	40
Jack Bushnell (10)	40
Laura Jones (10)	41
Grace O'Hagan (10)	41

Langney Primary School, Eastbourne

Parish CE Primary School, Bromley

Megan Wright (9)	64
Molly Margiotta (9)	64
Nilojana Nirmalan (9)	65
Henry Miller (7)	65
Earl Theo McInnis (9)	66
Sophie Evans (9)	66
Eliz Mullali (9)	67

Potley Hill Primary School, Yateley

Jamie Barker (9)	67
Paige Brown (10)	68
Euan O'Mahony (7)	68
Ellie White (9)	69
Georgia Warner (9)	69
Emily Mackie (10)	70
Kerrie Pither (10)	70
Charlie Smith (9)	71
Lauryn Lee Raymond (10)	71
Emily Hourahane (9)	72
Jake Maxwell (7)	72
Lucy Hagger (9)	73
Mason Lelliott (9)	73
Shaun Sims (11)	74
Charlotte Forshaw (9)	74
Christian Barrett (10)	75
Christopher Bates (9)	75
Ben Cook (10)	76
Sophie Langdon (9)	76
Lewis Rosier (10)	77
Jackson Bailey (9)	77
Lucy Allen (10)	78
Josh Morgan (10)	79
Samuel Morgan (10)	80
Courtney Chiles (9)	80
Charlotte Heape (8)	81
Liam Morgan (7)	81
Isabella Hart (8)	82
Jake Green (10)	82
Natasha Saunders (7)	83
William Wallace (9)	83
Charlotte Wetherell (9)	84

Colin Steer (9)   85
Claire Edwards (9)   86
Maddie Andrews (10)   86
Alicia Dallibar   87
Amy Herbert (9)   88
George Goodsell (10)   88
Jason Allen (9)   89
Connor Maxted (10)   89
Thomas Smallbone (10)   90
Benjamin Halvey (10)   91
Bethany Rosier (10)   92
Summer French (10)   93
Jordan Lambert (9)   94
Harry Bowman (10)   95
Ellen Pearce (9)   96
Callum Chappell (8)   96
Nathan Connolly (10)   97
Siân Wells (10)   97
Danielle Moir (9)   98
Alex Pritchard (10)   98
Thomas Kent (10)   99
Lucy Rampling (9)   99
Nathanael King (10)   100
Liam Cox (9)   101
Laurel Glazier (7)   102
Harry Butler (10)   102
Paige Calcott (9)   103
Victoria Herridge (9)   103
Anthony Slocombe (10)   104
Paris O'Keeffe (9)   105
Alex Richman (9)   106
Jade Maxwell (10)   107
Pratisha Bantawa (9)   108
Bethan Williams (10)   109
Calum O'Mahony (9)   110
Laura Drake (10)   111

St Fidelis Catholic School, Erith
Mary Okunsanwo ((8)   112
Rachel Brown (9)   112
Phoebe O'Reilly (7)   113

Isobel Pinto (10)	113
Chloe Huggon (8)	114
Melanie Andrade (9)	114
Faye Larkins (8)	115
Zarah Pinto (8)	115
Omoye Osebor (10)	116
Marianne Jennings (7)	116
Cristina Buscaglia (7)	117
Catherine Melder (10)	117
Rebecca Wheatley (8)	118
Tanya Nour (9)	118
Charlotte Rootsey (9)	119
Thomas Rawlings (10)	119
Hannah Akinshade (9)	120
Laura Burn (9)	120

Staunton & Corse School, Gloucester

Sophie Price (7)	121
Jack Collins (8)	121
Isobel Caine (7)	122
Laurie Cam (7)	122
Dino Bradford (7)	122
Abigail Ball (7)	123
Max Rayner (7)	123
Rowan Smith (6)	123
Matthew Cox (8)	124
Samuel Lane (7)	124
Chloe Cullen (8)	124

Westlea Primary School, Swindon

Kate Morrison (8)	125
Beth Adams (7)	125
Sophie Peart (9)	126
Marcus Bateman (10)	126
Faye Rogers (10)	127
Anna Waddington (10)	127
Tess Pringle (9)	128
Jack Adams (10)	128

The Poems

Swishy Fishy

Fish swim in the water, making a wish.
They swing their tail fins swish, swish, swish.
Eighteen fish went down to town.
Fish zoom through the tank up and down.
It gets very cold in winter,
Especially the filter.
Children follow their school lines.
Baby fish whine.
Fish have excellent minds.
Small fish use swimming trunks.
Fish don't sleep on bunks.
Little Sam was last in the race.
Fishy, pack your case.
Have a stretch, and then bend.
The end.

Sophie Lyons (8)

The Joy of Love

Love makes you feel calm.
It makes me joyful and happy.
Your heart makes a lovely shape
And makes me feel like a sweet chocolate cake.
Being hugged and loved.

It's like two hearts joined to one another.
And helps me feel sweet like a flower.
And my heart then has the power.
To connect to everyone.
In the joyful life I have.

N Latto (10)

Fruit Bowl

Grapes are great and make you graceful
Bananas come in bunches and make you bendy,
Apples are delicious and give you a good appetite,
Peaches are perfect, and come in a punnet,
Figs make you jig, and you get fit, quicker,
Crisps make you crazy,
Chocolate makes you lazy,
That's why I have fruit to munch at every lunch.

Rebecca Pentland (8)

Autumn

Icy frost walking in the autumn air,
Red leaves falling from the cold autumn tree.
Winning conkers celebrating their win,
Wild squirrels running in their huts.
Colourful fireworks cycling in the air.

Blue rain floating to the ground,
Mud hopping through the soft soil.
Loud carnival sounds in the air,
School swimming in the deep, deep pool.
Crazy Bonfire Night writing.

Jack Sloper (10)
Burbage Primary School, Marlborough

Autumn Poem

Mystical mud is hopped over,
Fireworks blazing in the sky.

Red squirrels hide their nuts in the frosty ground,
And the winter carnivals trundle along through the night.

Rhys Appleton (10)
Burbage Primary School, Marlborough

Autumn Time

Sparkling frost slipping around,
Golden brown leaves dancing on the ground,
Perfect crops swaying in the green fields,
Colourful fireworks exploding in the sky!

Magical carnivals floating along in the breeze,
Excited schools celebrating, harvest is here,
Bonfires crackling as the wood is burning,
Autumn is here, *hoora*y!

Rebecca Grist (10)
Burbage Primary School, Marlborough

Jenga

I live in a cupboard.
I can smell wine and vodka on the bottom shelf.
People think I am an old-fashioned game,
I am as old as the tree I came from.
My biggest fear is toppling over,
Will they play again?
My name is Jenga.

Rachel Valiant (10)
Burbage Primary School, Marlborough

What Am I?

I live in a school
I can hear children learning
I have a light in me
I am as old as the classroom I live in
I remember the teacher spinning me
I am afraid of my light going out
I wish to see my brothers; the sun and the moon
I overhear about geography
I do not understand why people spin me.

George Feakes (10)
Burbage Primary School, Marlborough

What Am I?

I live in a place with trees,
I taste lush green grass,
I can transform into anything.
My body is as cold as the Earth,
I remember more things like me,
I'm afraid of being seen.
My dream is to have more like me,
I've overheard a shotgun fire,
I don't understand why people don't believe in me.

I am a . . . unicorn.

Amy Clarke (10)
Burbage Primary School, Marlborough

Autumn

Dripping rain floating down from the sky.
Harvest is jumping into life,
Where we give food to the poor and the old.
Crunching leaves skipping along the ground.
Frost is pushing its way through.

Brown conkers banging in a fight,
Red squirrels jogging to collect nuts,
Bare trees running into winter,
Colourful loud fireworks,
Diving back down to Earth.

Hannah Goodall (10)
Burbage Primary School, Marlborough

Boon Went To The Moon

A highwayman called Boon
Wanted to go to the moon.

He hid behind a cloud in the sky
Until a shuttle came by.

He jumped on board
And swung his sword.

He shouted, 'Stand and deliver'
Take me to the moon!

The astronaut took Boon
To the moon

Boon slipped on some ice
And fell into a crater!

Jack Forgacs (8)
Burbage Primary School, Marlborough

Autumn Poem

Squirrels swimming through golden
Brown leaves that filled the air.
Leaves walking through the air,
As they calmly hit the ground
And are reunited.
Brothers and sisters
Rot into the ground.

Luke Callaghan (10)
Burbage Primary School, Marlborough

The Highwayman

There was a highwayman called Tom
He always forgot his gun.
He lived in a bush and jumped out at travellers
And bellowed, 'Stand and deliver!'
Tom got cut right through his heart.
Tom got tied to a tree
He was untied by someone,
But he didn't know who!
He turned into a ghost
And followed the travellers in a ghostly move.
He went over to them and shouted in a ghostly voice,
'Stand and deliver,' again.
The travellers tried to shoot him
But they couldn't see him.

Tom Teagle (8)
Burbage Primary School, Marlborough

A Highwayman On The Moon

A highwayman called Boon
Wanted to go to the moon
He hid behind a cloud in the sky
Until a shuttle came by.
Jumped on board and swung his sword
He shouted, 'Stand and deliver.
Take me to the moon.'
The astronaut gave him a parachute
And Boon jumped off the moon.

Aled Jenkins (8)
Burbage Primary School, Marlborough

Wild Child

Have you ever been to Loch Ness,
Or read about a Greek goddess?
Done a wheelie on a bike,
Ever met a wasp you like?
Written a story, written a play?
Had a friend in Webbs Way?
Tripped into a garden bin?
Ever seen your teacher win?
Read a thousand books?
Swum in a brook?
Gone fishing with your dad?
Then gone completely mad?
Cooked a cake with your mum?
Called your friend who wouldn't come?
Have you ever?

William Scott (9)
Burbage Primary School, Marlborough

Wild Child

Have you ever teased your brother?
Had an argument with your mother?
Swum in the sea at night?
Had a big cat fight?
Been on the moon?
Got a new spoon?
Ever eaten frogs' legs?
Ever been a man who begs?
Have you ever?

Sara Churnside (9)
Burbage Primary School, Marlborough

Wild Child

Have you ever jumped so high?
Have you eaten a custard pie?
Have you made a great big sigh?
Seen a dove flying the sky?
Picked a daisy, picked a rose?
Pushed your fingers down to your toes?
Flown a kite?
Got in a fight?
Made a story? (But can you write?)
Seen an amazing sight?
Have you played the violin?
Put the rubbish in the bin?
Fallen over, cut your knee?
Seen a monkey saying *wheee*?
Have you ever?

Bethany Martin (9)
Burbage Primary School, Marlborough

Fun With Couplets

Have you ever,
     Jumped out of a plane?
     Driven down a lane?
     Seen an active volcano?
     Seen a cheetah go slow?
     Seen a pointy tower?
     Picked a gigantic flower?
     Ridden a turtle, ridden a pig?
     Worn your gran's wig?
     Have you ever?

Oscar Palmer (9)
Burbage Primary School, Marlborough

Wild Child

Have you ever been into space?
Have you ever won a race?
Have you ever worn a wig
Or eaten in a big fat pig?
Ever won a competition?
Ever gone out on a mission?
Ever eaten fish?
Made a really special wish?
Seen a lark, seen a shark?
Played in the dark and touched a spark
Have you ever drunk seawater?
Or smacked your daughter?
Have you ever had a fight
Or burnt your finger on a light?
Have you ever?

India Kirby (9)
Burbage Primary School, Marlborough

Happy Days

Have you ever ridden a horse?
Fallen in a patch of gorse?
Got stuck in a tree?
Run down a slide shouting, 'Yippee!'
Gutted a fish,
Put it on a dish?
Hugged your dog?
Rescued a rather bedraggled frog?
Held a butterfly, held a moth?
Seen a painting of Van Gogh?
Have you ever?

Elizabeth Rawlinson (9)
Burbage Primary School, Marlborough

Done It Before . . .

Have you ever painted yourself?
Had lots of money or lots of wealth?
Caught a fish?
Broken a dish?
Cut your own hair?
Found a big lair?
Run a huge mile?
Read a secret file?
Eaten a doughnut, eaten a bun?
Missed out on loads of fun?
Ridden a bike?
Had a mud ball fight?
Ripped your clothes?
Picked a rose?
Been chased by a dog?
Run in a bog?
Have you ever?

Joanna Buck (9)
Burbage Primary School, Marlborough

Wild Child

Have you ever,
Kissed a frog?
Ridden a hog?
Swum in the sea?
Eaten a mushy pea?
Been a man?
Made a fan?
Driven a truck, driven a car?
Eaten a chocolate bar?
Have you ever?

Tilly Volant (9)
Burbage Primary School, Marlborough

Let's Call It A Day

Have you ever eaten a bun?
Have you ever drunk a bottle of rum?
Been to the moon?
Seen the bottom of a baboon?
Ever seen a goat?
Ever sat in a boat?
Have you ever cut your knee?
Ever flown with a bee?
Have you picked flowers?
Heard the words 'April showers'?
Ever been on a mission?
Ever been to an optician?
Been to Mars?
Eaten lots of Galaxy bars?
Have you ever?

Emily Hamill-Loader (9)
Burbage Primary School, Marlborough

Happy Days

Have you ever cracked your head?
Have you ever slept in a bed?
Had a brother?
Kissed your mother?
Had a sweet, then another?
Ever liked your teacher?
Seen a creature?
Even filmed a feature?
Have you ever?

Victoria Pierce-Jones (9)
Burbage Primary School, Marlborough

Fun With Couplets

Have you ever slept with a cuddly bear?
Have you ever had a cousin called Claire?
Have you seen a cow?
Had a ride on a plough?
Ever travelled in space?
Ever done the human race?
Got stuck in a slide?
Fallen over with pride?
Have you ever had a smelly foot?
Have you ever got covered in soot?
Have you ever?

Olivia Pierce-Jones (9)
Burbage Primary School, Marlborough

Wild Child

Have you ever
Been on a boat,
Or eaten a big bar of soap?
Eaten glue?
Flushed your face down the loo?
Have you ever broken your head?
Or cracked a piece of lead?
Eaten a blueberry, eaten some toast?
Had a friend that likes to boast?
Read a book?
Got covered in soot?
Have you ever?

Tilley Oliver (9)
Burbage Primary School, Marlborough

Fun With Couplets

Have you ever worn a hat in bed?
Have you ever broken a pencil lead?
Have you ever played with your pet?
Have you ever got the carpet wet?
Have you ever drunk some milk, drunk some tea?
Have you ever squashed a big pea?
Ever picked a flower?
Had super power?
Picked a rose?
Messed up your clothes?
Pulled out the bath plug?
Seen a slug?
Run a mile
With a big smile?
Have you ever?

Emily Wren (9)
Burbage Primary School, Marlborough

Have You Ever . . .

Have you ever ridden a bike?
Have you ever had a great big fright?
Ever had a dog?
Fallen in a bog?
Eaten a sausage?
You could have a cottage,
Ever had a kite?
Ever been in a fight?
Have you ever?

Alex Parmenter (9)
Burbage Primary School, Marlborough

Crazy Things

Have you ever
Been called Fred
Then been told to go to bed?
Have you ever eaten a log
Then bought a dog?
Have you ever laid in grass
Then cleaned brass?
Have you ever stayed alive
Then fallen in a hive?
Have you ever seen the Queen
Then been mean?
Have you ever had a brother
Then gone out with your mother?
Have you ever?

Emily Daubney (9)
Burbage Primary School, Marlborough

Have You Ever . . .

Have you ever played the flute?
Worn a shiny music suit?
Jumped into space?
Drawn a clown face?
Written a book, written a play?
Had a very nice day?
Been in the sea?
Smiled with glee?
Kissed a frog?
Ridden a dog?
Picked a rose?
Had a doze?
Have you ever?

Charlotte Bailey (9)
Burbage Primary School, Marlborough

My Dog

My dog would be my furry alarm clock
My dog would be nice and fluffy
My dog would come in its own basket
My dog would have a red and blue collar
Saying Bruce the Labrador
My dog would have colourful blue eyes
My dog would have a fluffy, shiny, golden coat
My dog would be really clever and able to cook tea
To give me and my mum a break
My dog would even be able to beat me in a running race
And that would be the dog for me!

Ben Crane (11)
Hordle Walhampton School, Lymington

Guy Fawkes

In 1605
King James was alive
There was treason around in the air,
Guy Fawkes was a man
Who came up with a plan
To send Parliament up with a flare.
The match was ready,
Guy said, 'Steady.'
The soldiers burst in
They arrested him
They said he was destined to hang
They were hung, drawn and quartered
They were really quite slaughtered

And no one cared.

Grace Murray (9)
Hordle Walhampton School, Lymington

My Dog

My dog was always there for me
Waiting by the door
He waited for his bone
While I was on the phone
His name was Joey
He loved my friend Zoe
And he didn't mind what I did
Around the kitchen he slid
On the tiles
Round and round
It made me smile,
Until he found the biscuits
He waited there for a while
His girlfriend's name was Jessie
She was a sheepdog and his bezzie
But my dog isn't here anymore
I miss him lots
Life's a bore
I wish he were here
Waiting for me by the door
When I get home from school
Waiting for his bone
And being my friend
While I'm all alone
He's in a better place now
Looking down on me
For when I'm in trouble
He's there at the double
So I'm never lonely.

Eleanor Taylor (11)
Hordle Walhampton School, Lymington

My Hotel

If you stay around
You will spin around
Yeah spin around
In my hotel
In my hotel

If you stay around
You will play around
Yeah play around
In my motel
In my motel

If you stay around
There are things to see
And things to do
In my hotel
In my hotel

If you stay around
You may come around
A lot of sound at night
In my motel
In my motel

You may find at half-past nine
A gazelle
In my hotel
In my hotel
Yeah!

Oliver Joy (9)
Hordle Walhampton School, Lymington

Gallipoli

Sunrise,
Our crafts were silhouetted,
On the horizon.
Those Turks started firing
On our small boats.
We landed on the sands,
As Mr Churchill does say,
Many of us on our deathbeds.

Here, on these shining sands,
Many of my comrades thought this fun,
We began a heroic assault,
But many knew there was a fault.
Our ships tried to cover us,
But our commanders made such a fuss,
O'er a failed landing.

We were evacuated,
And much we were deflated,
The Turks bombarded our vessels,
And many ships were lost,
And thrice as many lives,
Were lost.

William Lee (10)
Hordle Walhampton School, Lymington

Autumn

Yellow, orange, red, gold and brown leaves
Scattered along the ground,
Bare trees swaying.
Animals preparing
For their long winter hibernation.
Hot sunny days with a crisp of winter coming.
Migration of birds flying south.
The winter breeze is coming once again.

Lilly Mann (8)
Hordle Walhampton School, Lymington

Dragons

If you walk into a dragon's den
Before you can say 'then',
You've been gobbled up, bones and all.

But a dragon is not always small
Some are big, some are tiny
Some are brave, some are whiny
Some are scaly, some are hairy
Some are wimps and want to be a fairy
All the dragons in the world have fiery breath,
With their scaly skin and many chins
They're very unusual creatures
With very unusual features
But all the dragons in the world
Would like to munch on you!

James Cockayne (9)
Hordle Walhampton School, Lymington

Guy Fawkes

Remember, remember,
Guy Fawkes had a plot to slot
Some gunpowder
Into the houses of Parliament

The guards found him
They tried to surround him
Guy Fawkes was caught
Even though he fought

Guy Fawkes lied
Then Fawkes died
Then he went down in history
Because of the mystery
Remember, remember the fifth of November.

Alexander McGrigor (9)
Hordle Walhampton School, Lymington

Bounty Hunters

Most bounty hunters have spaceships,
Boba Fett had Slave 1,
And it would have blaster cannons,
With a speed of bike.

Jabba the Hutt is their leader,
But he's much too mean.
Some of them found lightsabers,
And some have blaster rifles.

They are very important people,
Most from Tatoinne.
Some are even cloned,
Normally Jango, but Boba can be cloned.

They all kill for money,
Except Han Solo.
He turned evil,
And I say he went mad!

Henry Marden (9)
Hordle Walhampton School, Lymington

Where I Like To 'Liv'

Ponies, ponies
Galloping through
Moonlight
The forest in the dark

Trees, trees
Waving in the wind
Their leaves falling in all different colours
And other shades

People, people
Walking in the village
Talking in the shops
And munching chips and chocs.

Olivia 'Liv' Williams (8)
Hordle Walhampton School, Lymington

Football

Goal!
Henry, Rooney and plenty more,
These are the ones who know how to score.
From short-range volleys to 40 yard shots,
If you can shoot like that you can be one of the tops.

Oh no!
There are own goals as well,
Though sometimes it's hard to tell,
But Jimmie Trayoras clever roulette
The problem is, it went in his own net.

To be the best is hard to do,
Though you can win, draw and lose,
But if you keep your head high and try your best,
To be one of the greats, you might just get.

Lewis Marden (10)
Hordle Walhampton School, Lymington

Sports

I have a talent for cricket
Even though I am a girl
You have to get your head around the game
If you want a wicket.

I have a talent for rugby
It's a muddy game
Wet and soggy, carry on anyway
Get tries and win the game.

I have a talent for netball
It's a busy and hot game
Get the ball and shoot some hoops.

I have a talent for hockey
I love hockey
Everyone thinks hockey is fun and dynamic.

Victoria Childs (10)
Hordle Walhampton School, Lymington

The Tree

Thin, bony branches
Seeping from a dark hole
A glaring moon
Bright, but without soul.

Towering above me,
As tall as a waterfall,
Leaves once green,
The roots unseen.

A chilly wind from the west
Demolishes the solitary leaf,
I watched it as far as my eye could see,
Never to be viewed again.

Beckoning fingers
Spreading through the foliage
Establishing communication
Striving to touch me.

The spindly fingers pointing south
The never-ending wind still blowing
I suddenly felt a chill on my leg
I peered down and spied a branch.

Wrapping rapidly around my leg,
Straining and struggling,
Tighter and tighter
The tree closes in.

Holly Nicholls (10)
Hordle Walhampton School, Lymington

Horses And Dogs

Snuff is my pony
He's in the field
All lonely
He is great at jumping
But forever bumping
Into trees.

Bounty is my auntie's dog
She is black and beautiful
And she is active
She is a cocker spaniel.

Pickles is Gemma's pony
She loves her,
Rides her,
And jumps her.

Inca is my family's
And mine
She is a German shepherd
She always takes her time
But I love her.

Georgina Lewis (10)
Hordle Walhampton School, Lymington

Dragons

Dragons, dragons large or wide
Flaming eyes and rotten teeth
Emerald and sapphire
Shimmering colours

Made to kill people, swallow them whole
Destroying castles, living in caves
Fire-breathing, scaly tails
Frying knights like beans in a can

Charred bones around their lairs
Flaming forests, full of death
Rotten breath
Smelling of human flesh

But up comes a wave,
A huge tsunami, sent from the gods
Drowning the dragons
Killing them instantly

'Hooray,' say the kings
'The dragons are dead!'
Miles away a dragon snores
Lying on eggs soon to hatch . . .

Thomas Shakespeare (10)
Hordle Walhampton School, Lymington

Sports

Cricket's the best,
It's the most fun,
Runs scored
Wickets taken
A new batsman has arrived.

Now it's rugby,
Huge people, tiny people
All different sizes,
Release your anger,
Come on let's see what you've got.

It's hockey now,
Flying sticks
Balls shooting about you,
Beaten one defender, and two
He shoots, he scores

Hit the target, it's shooting,
Lie down, the gun's loaded
Aim and fire,
It's a good shot; it's a bull,
The final mark out of 100,
Is 89
A very good round.

Louis Ambrose (11)
Hordle Walhampton School, Lymington

Animals

Animals, animals you find them almost everywhere,
Sometimes underground, in the sea
Or even in the air!

As for those cats with a million spots,
Like those leopards and the cheetahs,
But not forgetting the majestic ocelots!

There is only one left to talk about,
Its roar as loud as 10 human shouts,
Its bones are as strong as iron,
Have you guessed it yet?
It's a *lion!*

Is there a soul brave enough to confront this beast?
Who is not afraid to be turned into a kitty feast?
I need someone who is strong and steady,
Well then, are you ready?

Harry Vokins (11)
Hordle Walhampton School, Lymington

Winter

Cold and chilly, but happy am I,
Because winter has arrived.
The wind is blowing,
The autumn's going,
And the snow is falling fast.

I put on my hat, scarf and gloves,
To play out in the snow,
We make snowmen and ice domes,
Then we go back home.

Another good thing that you should know,
Is that Christmas is in winter,
Not in summer, autumn or spring.
Christmas is in . . .
Winter!

Marsha Allan-Burns (9)
Hordle Walhampton School, Lymington

Sport

Rugby is a great sport,
Some people say it is rubbish and snort,

Football is dynamic and fun,
It is also very skilful,

In cricket,
You need to get the wicket,

Tennis is an energetic sport,
You need to beat your rivals on the court,

In hockey you need good ball skills,
You need to manoeuvre the opposition,

In sport you need to practice,
If you don't then do not gloat,
If you are not passionate about what you do,
You will not succeed in what you play,
Sport is a great thing to do,
There are all types of sports,
From fencing to athletics.

Conor Bevens (10)
Hordle Walhampton School, Lymington

Black As The Night

Black as the night
Swiftly flies the shadow
Black as the night
Clawing through the trees
Black as the night
Brightly shine the eyes
Black as the night
Creeping stealthily
Black as the night
Panther!

Grace Taylor (9)
Hordle Walhampton School, Lymington

My Cousin Laura And Me

I really do like Laura
And she really does like me
And that's just as well
Because, we're cousins, you see

I like it when she comes to stay
For a week or two or three
We have such fun together
My cousin Laura and me

We like to play down on the beach
Especially by the sea
Collecting lots of pretty shells
My cousin Laura and me

We like to dress up as princesses
We're not much into climbing a tree
We'd like to live in a castle
My cousin Laura and me

We sing and dance and have such fun
Until it's time for tea
Maybe we'll be on stage one day
My cousin Laura and me

When it's time for her to go
A tear in my eye you'll see
We really are the best of friends
My cousin Laura and me.

Chloe Larby (8)
Hordle Walhampton School, Lymington

Seaside

Sand squidging beneath my feet,
Lots and lots of ice cream to eat,
Waves hitting against the rocks
Seagulls flying by the dock,
Happy smiling faces, playing in the sand,
Lots and lots of people listening to the band,
Punch and Judy puppet shows, entertaining the crowd.
Claps and squeals of sheer delight,
People cheering out loud.
Ice cream kiosks all around,
Choice is hard to make,
Ninety-nines and *flakes* and cones,
What will the children take?
Buying buckets, spades, flags and bright windmills,
Forever building sandcastles, moats and hills,
Donkey rides, tourist attractions, Red Arrows fly,
Daring displays decorating the sky!
Glittering sand, stones and shells,
The rush of the waves from those beautiful bells.
Seaweed, suncream, sandwiches and sea,
This is what a sunny seaside means to me.

Arabella Watkiss (10)
Hordle Walhampton School, Lymington

Ponies Are Great

Long ago
Ponies went to war
Some were injured

Modern times
Life is fine
Ponies gallop
All the time

Kept in stables
Or nearby fields
We are able
To feed them meals

Jumping fences
Breathing fast
To begin with
We are home at last.

Mattea Pauc (8)
Hordle Walhampton School, Lymington

Surfing

You wait for a wave
Find a great wave
You paddle it
You catch it
You stand up
You feel a blue-green wave
On the crest of a wave
You feel like you're on top of the world
You feel powerful.

Frazer Poulter (8)
Hordle Walhampton School, Lymington

What Shall I Do?

I don't know what to do
Poems to write, oh what a delight!
I don't know what to do

What to do, what to do
With a poem to write
Oh I wish I were a great poet

With things to do and things to write
I'd rather just be out of sight

I need some ideas, a lot of ideas
Like shapes, fairies, oh these are my worst fears

Ideas with ponies, dogs and maybe a few cats
Ideas with doors, curtains and even some mats.

Anya Jackson (9)
Hordle Walhampton School, Lymington

My Magic Box

(Inspired by 'Magic Box' by Kit Wright)

I will put in my box . . .
The scale of the dragon,
The honey of the bee,
The love of my heart,
And the wind of the sea.
The glow of a star
The sun and moon
The pyramids of Egypt
And a magic balloon.

There is nothing too big
And nothing too small
I can put it all in,
No matter how tall!

Valentina Sassow (8)
Hordle Walhampton School, Lymington

Stallion Being Caught In A Storm

Rearing and bucking
The sound of his hooves
On the stone paths
Coming down lanes

Sweating like mad
They're stealing tonight,
That's what they are doing
I'll give them a fright

I tack up my horse
So quickly I shake,
Get on like lightning
And race out the gate.

I hear the squeak of the saddle
The flick of the reins
The jangle of the bit
And the sound of the whip.

I'm catching up!
I'm catching up!
I've caught them
I've caught them

Hooray! Hooray!
I've got them at last
I'll take them to court
They will be sorry!

My horse is sweating
He has run for his life
His numnah is soaked.
He has saved the stallion in the storm!

Katie Newsom (9)
Hordle Walhampton School, Lymington

A Cross-Country Run

The day of the race has finally come
I'm warming up and am ready to run
I stretch my legs and touch my toes
My fitness is high, I hope it shows

They call my name and I walked to the line,
My tummy is turning which is a good sign
I crouch like a tiger and am ready to pounce
The whistle blows and I hear lots of shouts

I'm off like the wind, just watch me go
But I tell myself, 'Go slow, go slow.'
I'm running, I'm running but I must keep it slow
The race is not over I've a long way to go

Squelch goes the mud, splash goes a paddle
Crack goes a stick and we're all in a muddle
I'm panting, I'm panting, my breath's running out
'You're about halfway,' I hear my friend shout

A boy comes from behind and pushes me aside
I fall in the mud, I could have cried
I'm panting, I'm panting my breath's running out
There's mud on my knees, this is what it's about

Oh good I'm coming fifth, no fourth, no third
I look around and see a rare bird
The boy who pushed me is up in front
I see him give another boy a shunt

I see the finish line, it's up ahead
'Go, go, go,' shouts my best friend Ted
I'm sprinting, I'm sprinting, I've put on a burst
Oh my goodness, I'm coming second, no I'm first!

Posy Hewitt (9)
Hordle Walhampton School, Lymington

Football

Football is a team game
You have to pass in football
If you don't pass
Your team will lose the ball

The whole idea of football
Is to score goals
If you score enough goals
You will win the match

Once my teammate passed to me
Then I scored a goal
But it did not count
Because I was offside

So when you play football
Try to score some goals
But also try
Not to be offside!

Keir Amyes-Headley (9)
Hordle Walhampton School, Lymington

Sport

Cricket is a sport
Where you bowl the ball,
It hits the bat,
And hopefully goes for four

Rugby is a sport,
Where you dip and dive,
Don't get tackled,
And hope to score the try.

Athletics is a sport,
With jumping, running and throwing,
Gold, silver and bronze medals,
And the last place in tears.

Felix Ambrose (9)
Hordle Walhampton School, Lymington

Sharks

Some sharks are big
Some sharks are small
Some sharks are vicious
Some sharks are tall
Some sharks have two fins
Some have four
I know some that know how to open a door!
Some sharks are round, some weigh a pound
Some sharks are large, some are un-found
Some sharks have big teeth, some make gore
Some sharks are fit, fall like water balls
Some sharks eat fish, one ate Paul
Most sharks eat seals, some play with balls,
Sharks are scary, some can eat you!
Some may bite you, even you, Paul.

James Wood (9)
Hordle Walhampton School, Lymington

Sailing

I love to sail upon the seas,
With whistling winds,
With trembling sails,
To wrestle the mainsail,
The unforgiving wind does whine,
The crew and I, as skipper,
Find it hard to keep her.

This is a race,
A big race,
We want to win,
But,
The raging wind makes it almost impossible,
As we lose places.

Tim Morgan (9)
Hordle Walhampton School, Lymington

Midnight Spirits

Spirits dancing everywhere
I watched them all around me, not a moment to spare
Surrounding me with their magical light
I stared up at the clock, it was midnight.

As they started to dance
The moon came out
From a distance I heard a shout
I didn't know what it was
Could it be something for the Wizard of Oz?

I looked around for a long time
One of them was holding a chime
I'm glad I didn't get near
Because I could have broken my ear

I started to get really scared
Before, I really didn't care
I ran to the house and up the stairs
Then I looked out the window to see the spirits' glares.

Eliza Cudmore (8)
Hordle Walhampton School, Lymington

A Story That Happened Long Ago In A World Far Away

In days of old when dragons lived,
When dwarfs could mine their mighty mines,
And knights went into battle shining
A wizard at his table sat.

The wizard conjured pixies all
He raised a stick and threw it down.
He shouted words of magic loud
And out came elves one and all.

The elves raised their swords and shouted
Words of praise to their wizard lord,
He shouted words to marching elves
Marching to the goblin herd.

Where they raised their swords and charged.
They clashed with them, swords and shields
Fought for days, 'til heard the elf shout
Words of triumph; they cried with happiness.

Through the light and back to their world.

Hugo Walters (10)
Hordle Walhampton School, Lymington

It's A Try

Passing down the line
Swishing through the field
Dodging, darting
Going faster and faster
I love to play
I really, really do
Wind through my hair
Tackling hard
The ball pops out of the scrum
Pounding down the blind side
Going faster and faster
Spinning out to the fly half
Catching in the air
Gliding and sliding
Finally it's there
Diving over the line
Touching down with a flourish
It's a try!

Joseph Holland (9)
Hordle Walhampton School, Lymington

Shark

Deadly, strong, ferocious, mean
Killer, creepy, fast, ambushes
Sensitive, fat, big, sharp teeth
Destructive, dangerous, ambushes
Living killer patrols the sea

Deadly shark, ferocious, mean
Swimming through the sea
Killer, creepy, big teeth
Sensitive to the sea, killer
Creepy, big, sharp teeth
Sensitive, fat, ambushes.

Theo Seely (8)
Hordle Walhampton School, Lymington

My Onomatopoeia Poem

Splish, splash, splosh,
Time to have a wash.
Soaked in mud
The rugby ball goes thud.
Tripped on my lace,
Fell on my face.
Mr Reed groaned
And the crowd moaned
'We need that try
Why? oh why
Did you slip and slide?
You could have scored one with a glide.'
We lost the game.
What a shame,
I hope I will not get the blame!

Jasper Slawson (9)
Hordle Walhampton School, Lymington

The Tree

The tree feels little bugs crawling up his trunk
like tiny flies jumping on frogs . . .

He thinks of lots of children and robins
playing on him in the sun . . .

He hears the blue tits cheeping
whilst he watches foxes pounce on rabbits . . .

He sees the children playing 'it'
as he stands tall in his ground . . .

He smells the scent of fresh air
surrounding him whilst he grows.

He tastes dust and air from all around . . .

Lucy Edwards (10)
Kempshott Junior School, Basingstoke

The Tree

The tree feels the burning hot sun
Shrivelling up all his lush green leaves
Like some wet washing-up on the line.
The tree slowly opens his eyes
To find a lovely cold river
Getting burned up in the sun.
The tree looks up and feels
A bird poke him as he
Tries to make a nest.
The tree can feel an animal
Hitting his roots as it
Tries to make a new home.
The tree smells some
Of his sap oozing out of
His trunk where a woodpecker
Has chipped through his bark.
The tree, who has children,
Playing around in his arms
Which gives him joy and pleasure.

Liam Askew
Kempshott Junior School, Basingstoke

Rationing

No butter, no bacon
No lard, no margarine
Just one shilling's worth of meat
And not much cheese
No tea, no coffee, no wonderful things
Just a lump of sugar and no jam
No bananas, no oranges, no trendy things.
Rationing!

Jack Bushnell (10)
Kempshott Junior School, Basingstoke

The Tree

The tree feels a bird making a nest to raise her children.
He can see children throwing his yellow, brown and red leaves in a
grassy field.
His hearing tells him that the birds are chirping and children talking.
A small child is trying to climb the tree but he is not tall enough yet.
The air is beautiful and fresh after the grass has been cut, the tree
can taste and smell it.
A squirrel is clambering over the rough, mossy bark to get to the top
of the tall tree.
In the wind his long twisted branches are swaying.
The tree feels happy and useful.
When the children go back into class it is quiet once more.

Laura Jones (10)
Kempshott Junior School, Basingstoke

A Poem To Be Spoken Silently

(Based on 'A Poem to be Spoken Silently' by Pie Corbett)

It was so silent that I heard a mouse tiptoe
across my carpet as I was fast asleep . . .

It was so still that I felt my floorboards crack
when an ant tiptoed along them . . .

It was so calm that I heard the blossom
grow as the leaves fell . . .

It was so peaceful that I sensed the bees
making honey in their beehive . . .

It was so quiet that I heard a butterfly
flutter in the sunset . . .

Grace O'Hagan (10)
Kempshott Junior School, Basingstoke

The Tree

The tree smiles as he overlooks flowery green fields
With New Forest foals galloping through.
As he opens his eyes wider
The warm summer sun gleams through his branches
Heating him slowly with only his leaves for shade.
The tree opens his mouth as sticky toffee sap dribbles down his trunk
Tickling him until a berry bursts to wash it away.
As a squirt of juice squeezes into his mouth
He stretches his arms and says, 'Mmmm.'
The tree feels happy and free.

Sally Owens (10)
Kempshott Junior School, Basingstoke

A Poem To Be Spoken Silently

(Based on 'A Poem to be Spoken Silently' by Pie Corbett)

It was so silent that I heard nothing but the
wind waving through the trees . . .

It was so calm that I felt the butterflies
escaping from their cocoon . . .

It was so harsh that I sent the deer
drinking quietly from a deep pool.

It was so silent that I heard the leaves fall
from an oak tree getting ready for autumn . . .

It was so hushed that I sensed a cat
bathing in the sun, spending the last few
minutes of his day.

Ruby Felton (10)
Kempshott Junior School, Basingstoke

The Tree

The tree can see sheep grazing on green grass
He hears blue tits sing and wind blow against the leaves
He feels beetles clawing their way up his back
He smells lavender blowing in the breeze
He touches the soil which is cold on his feet
He tastes the sap dripping from his bark
He thinks he's in a wonderful place.

George Steel (10)
Kempshott Junior School, Basingstoke

The Tree

The tree sees masses of mountainous rocks
high up in the misty depths of
an exploding volcano . . .

The tree hears thundering explosions
of toxic gas and molten rock,
spreading throughout the rocky space.

The tree smells piles of dirt and ash
covering his old and stubby body.

The tree tastes not a drop of
glistening water from the very top
of the thin mountain stream.

The tree feels cold and lonely
in the place of fire and
disastrous weather.

The tree thinks of a colourful horizon,
full of trees bursting with life
from a rocky cage trapping his dream.

Adam Cook (10)
Kempshott Junior School, Basingstoke

A Poem To Be Spoken Silently

(Based on 'A Poem to be Spoken Silently' by Pie Corbett)

It was so tranquil that I heard
the cat's claws scrape the wood
on a stormy night . . .

It was so still that I sensed
the raindrops freeze,
on the night of a hailstorm . . .

It was so silent that I heard
the blood drip from my elbow,
like rain from the clouds . . .

It was so calm that I heard
my stomach rumble in the night,
like stumbling through the jungle . . .

It was so hushed that I felt
the sun give off its beams of light,
just like a torch . . .

Siobhan Harrison (10)
Kempshott Junior School, Basingstoke

Rationing

No coffee, no tea,
No chocolate, no cheese!
No bacon, no sausage,
No proper goods on our plates.

No warmth, no health,
No comfort, no ease!
No proper feeling in any way.

No light, no dark,
No wasps, no bees!
No birds, no leaves,
No quiet, no peace!
Rationing!

Lewis Parker-Allen (10)
Kempshott Junior School, Basingstoke

The Tree

The tree feels the leopard-white snowflakes
fall off his evergreen leaves
and melt down and off his feet.
He sees the children laughing
as the snowflakes are freezing in their eyes.
He touches his smooth, soft coat of bark
cracking as the atmosphere gets colder and colder.
He hears the children laughing and giggling
as they glide down the steep hill on their sledges
He tastes the soft, still snowflakes on his tongue.
He smells mince pies and roast dinners
on Christmas Eve and Christmas Day
and wishes he could share in the love and joy of others.

Zoe Swyny (10)
Kempshott Junior School, Basingstoke

The Tree

The tree opens his eyes
and sees in the distance small children
playing tag on a hot summer's day.
He feels left out
because he can't move one bit
to go and play with the small happy children.
He thinks about nothing
apart from moving
because he wants to play with someone.
When it's break or lunch
and the kids come out,
He loves it when the children say,
'Let's cool down under that tree's shadow.'
And that's what makes him feel special today.

Thomas Waite (10)
Kempshott Junior School, Basingstoke

A Poem To Be Spoken Silently

(Based on 'A Poem to be Spoken Silently' by Pie Corbett)

It was so silent that I heard
the birds singing
like a human being . . .

It was so peaceful that I heard
the grass swaying
like someone's hair blowing . . .

It was so still that I heard
the grasshoppers nattering
like a little field mouse chewing . . .

It was so peaceful that I heard
an owl twitter
in the moonlight sky . . .

It was so silent that I heard
a daddy-long-legs fly
like the gentle wind . . .

It was so hushed that I felt
a raindrop giggle
like a new beginning . . .

Samantha Benham (10)
Kempshott Junior School, Basingstoke

A Poem To Be Spoken Silently

(Based on 'A Poem to be Spoken Silently' by Pie Corbett)

It was so serene that I felt my sister
just waking up from her deep slumber. . .

It was so peaceful that I heard a newborn lamb
have its first breath . . .

It was so calm that I heard my brain snoring
like a cat next to a fire.

It was so tranquil that I felt my book
whispering to its neighbour,
'He's going to read me next.'

It was so still that I felt a snake
in a desert, shed his skin . . .

It was so quiet that I sensed the beetle
scuttle along in the newly wet grass . . .

It was so hushed that I heard a leaf falling
from the tree just like newspaper
falling on the ground . . .

Daniel Woolley (10)
Kempshott Junior School, Basingstoke

The Tree

The tree feels warm feeling like
hot chocolate running down his body.
The tree brushes the leaves
down him like snow falling
Down his back.
He stands watching the time
pass like watching a clock
go by in the distance.
Bugs crawl and slither
round his trunk like
itching on his skin.
He laughs at kids playing
nearby and rustles
his leaves in amusement.
He thinks of birds humming
on a branch
like singing in his mind.
The tree stands in his place
covering children from the sun
until he is old.
He stands leaning over us
for generations.

Leah Moore (10)
Kempshott Junior School, Basingstoke

A Poem To Be Spoken Silently

(Based on 'A Poem to be Spoken Silently' by Pie Corbett)

It was so silent that I heard
the feet of the bird pitter-patter
like hailstones in a thunderstorm . . .
It was so peaceful that I felt
the scab on my knee-cap peel off
like a sticker in a book . . .
It was so still that I sensed
a leaf from a tree falling
like a raindrop from the clouds . . .
It was so calm that I heard
an ant crawling up my leg
and whisper to its tribe,
'This is safe; she's still as a statue . . . '
It was so quiet that I heard
a pencil lead fall to the ground
like a man parachuting from a plane . . .
It was so serene that I sense
the trees swaying
like the fur of a tiger in the breeze . . .
It was so tranquil that I heard
the earth rotate on its axis
like a ball being kicked along the floor . . .

Aisha Gibson (10)
Kempshott Junior School, Basingstoke

A Poem To Be Spoken Silently

(Based on 'A Poem to be Spoken Silently' by Pie Corbett)

It was so silent that I heard
raindrops fall
like skaters on ice . . .

It was so still that I felt
my heart beat
like a wave of static in my body . . .

It was so hushed that I sensed
a spider spinning a web
like a lady knitting . . .

It was so quiet that I sensed
a frog leap gracefully
like a leaf slowly going down the river . . .

It was so tranquil that I heard
the beat of a butterfly's wings
as they hit together . . .

Daniel Stanway (10)
Kempshott Junior School, Basingstoke

A Poem To Be Spoken Silently

(Based on 'A Poem to be Spoken Silently' by Pie Corbett)

It was so peaceful that I heard
a baby in the womb
move in a deep sleep

It was so still that I heard
the first snowflake in winter

It was so calm I felt
a baby take his first steps
along the hallway of luck

It was so hushed that I sensed
the tide go in and out
across the sea

Molly Gardiner (10)
Kempshott Junior School, Basingstoke

A Poem To Be Spoken Silently

(Based on 'A Poem to be Spoken Silently' by Pie Corbett)

It was so quiet that I heard
the whisper of the wind
like he was carrying a secret message . . .

It was so calm that I heard
the footsteps of the ants
like I was there with them . . .

It was so peaceful that I felt
the rain trickling down to the ground
like spiders spinning a web . . .

It was so hushed that I sensed
that a baby had been born
like I knew where it was . . .

It was so tranquil that I heard
the songs of the birds miles away
like they were right next to me . . .

Connor Izzo & Lewis Wright (10)
Kempshott Junior School, Basingstoke

The Tree

The tree opens his eyes and sees a huge beach
The children playing in their swimming trunks
He hears shouting and screaming and laughter
While he's really lonely
He can smell seaweed, open water and sea
so he's really used to the smell.
The tree tastes sand and dust because of the wind from the sea.
He can feel the children in his branches playing;
It makes him feel wanted.
The tree thinks, *I want to live forever.*

Ellis Sloggett (10)
Kempshott Junior School, Basingstoke

A Poem To Be Spoken Silently

(Based on 'A Poem to be Spoken Silently' by Pie Corbett)

It was so peaceful that I heard
a raindrop fall like a feather
floating to the ground softly

It was so calm that I heard
leaves rustle like a paper bag
in the wind

It was so silent that I felt
a gust of wind
like a big snowstorm

It was so calm that I sensed
the grass swaying gently like a whisper,
in the air, that someone had said

It was so still that I heard
a bird's feet going pit-pat, pit-pat down the street
like a person opening a book.

Rebecca Hannah (10)
Kempshott Junior School, Basingstoke

A Poem To Be Spoken Silently

(Based on 'A Poem to be Spoken Silently' by Pie Corbett)

It was so calm that I heard
silver silk clouds walk on the sky . . .

It was so serene that I felt
a soft white wolf shiver in fear . . .

It was so hushed that I sensed
as soft shivering man pray for strength . . .

It was so peaceful that I heard
stones whisper to the mud, You're keeping me safe.'

It was so tranquil that I heard
a cry of joy from a baby looking at his mum for love . . .

It was so calm that I heard
the sound of a soul like the loving sounds of dreams . . .

It was so serene that I sensed
a thousand wars stop the dirty greed . . .

Greg Lee (10)
Kempshott Junior School, Basingstoke

The Tree

The tree feels his buds opening;
beautifying his outstretched arms.
The tree sees the squirrels playing, the foxes prowling,
the badgers sneaking and the bunnies hopping with joy.
He hears the children looking for him,
It makes him feel important.
He thinks his bark will protect him like a golden suit of armour.
The tree wakes up and tastes the fresh spring air
and eats up the sun's rays.
The children look up to him
for protection from the sun.
So, as he stands in his spot
watching everything change,
he happily protects the children with his arms.

When you go to see him now you will not be surprised
that he still stands in his spot
and will do so for many years to come.

Jack Bambridge (10)
Kempshott Junior School, Basingstoke

The Tree

The tree feels the grass so dry like hay.
He tastes the last of his sap
As he thinks to himself,
Soon I'll be gone because the cities are growing.
The tree sees the city growing wider.
What was once land is now sand from the building site.
The city is so noisy with buses and cars,
The tree can't hear farms or birds tweeting in the sky.
He now smells smoky air choking him.
He dreams of a time before cities.

Melissa Gartland (10)
Kempshott Junior School, Basingstoke

Eyes Tight Shut

With my eyes tight shut I can hear . . .

The breeze of a bird that flies above me,
A car hooting that is stuck in traffic,
Trying to get in front of it,
A bag rustling down the road to get my attention.

With my eyes tight shut I can hear . . .

Someone counting down the corridor, with happiness,
Laughing from the children in the hall,
Anxious talking from Mrs Banner, telling them to line up.

With my eyes tight shut I can hear . . .
A bird in the tree speaking words of kindness to his mates,
A train charging down the winding tracks,
Bumblebee flying around his words of wisdom.

Jake Skingle (9)
Langney Primary School, Eastbourne

Eyes Tight Shut

With my eyes tight shut I can hear . . .
People waiting anxiously for the traffic to move on.
Mrs Banner's beads rattling as she walks.
Bees buzzing along as happy as can be.

With my eyes tight shut I can hear . . .
Cars charging down the road, as fast as they can go.
The water from the fountain gracefully falling.
Teachers giggling loudly in the staffroom on their break.

With my eyes tight shut I can hear . . .
The office lady typing madly on the computer.
Faint footsteps in the background, but as quiet as can be.
Trees rustling calmly in the wind.

Leah Warren (9)
Langney Primary School, Eastbourne

Eyes Tight Shut

With my eyes tight shut I can hear . . .

Birds singing songs of happiness in the graceful winds,
A car zooming down the road, tooting its horn,
And a class shouting and learning.

With my eyes tight shut I can hear . . .

A gate screeching back and forth,
People talking loudly,
The warm buzzing of the bumblebee.

With my eyes tight shut I can hear . . .

A phone ringing madly,
The caretaker talking non-stop,
Somebody's tummy rumbling like a volcano ready to blow.

Christian Maynard (9)
Langney Primary School, Eastbourne

With My Eyes Tight Shut

I can hear . . .
Birds twittering in the deep blue sky
Cars *vroooming* across the pitch-black road
The copy machine making a shushing sound
The plain wood door creaking at school
Wind blowing everything in its path
Shoes stomping on the ground
Trees rustling in the breeze.

Jayden Webb (9)
Langney Primary School, Eastbourne

Eyes Tight Shut

With my eyes tight shut I can hear . . .

Birds singing a happy song, sweetly in the trees,
The wind whistling through my ears quietly,
And Mrs Compton's tummy rumbling angrily like a bear.

With my eyes tight shut I can hear . . .

Quiet breathing in and out, out and in,
The window cleaner banging on the windows,
And Mrs Banner shouting loudly at her class.

With my eyes tight shut I can hear . . .

The sound of a printer printing, *ch ch ch ch ch ch,*
And water trickling almost silently.

Jessica Deacon (9)
Langney Primary School, Eastbourne

With My Eyes Tight Shut

I can hear . . .
Birds screeching on top of the world
The wind slashing around and around
Ring, ring,
The door clashes open and shut
The beeping of a printer
And Mrs Banner going, '5, 4, 3, 2, 1.'

Declan Hoad (9)
Langney Primary School, Eastbourne

With My Eyes Tight Shut

I can hear the weary cry of the creaking door,
The echo of a pencil that fell on the playground.
Honking of road sweepers, arguing,
Loud voices of people talking,
The roaring of planes zooming over,
The tapping of a desk once forgotten,
Thundering footsteps in corridors,
The humming of the laminator,
Shuffling kids living in the streets,
Loud seagulls squawking far away,
A learning class answering their times tables.

Harry Watts (9)
Langney Primary School, Eastbourne

With My Eyes Tight Shut

With my eyes tight shut I can hear
Paper fluttering in the whistling wind,
Birds screeching in the clear blue sky,
And the mournful call of the door as it creaks shut.
With my eyes shut tight I can hear
A class chanting like a wind chime in the wind,
Wind whistling through the trees,
And bin men reversing noisily.
With my eyes tight shut
That is what I can hear.

Estella Moreno (9)
Langney Primary School, Eastbourne

With My Eyes Tight Shut

I can hear planes
Shooting through the sky.
The birds shrieking
Through the glittering sky
Sweeping up and down
Shouting as loudly as a lion's roar.
And cars rushing past.
Doors slamming like a volcano erupting.
Trees crackling like pencils dropping.

Georges Phillips (10)
Langney Primary School, Eastbourne

With My Eyes Tight Shut

I can hear . . .
The whooshing and swaying of the wind
Shoes squeaking, birds squawking
Pencil clanging, gate creaking,
Mmmmming of the laminator,
Shuffling along the floor
5, 4, 3, 2, 1 tapping
people chatting,
Lorry reversing,
Banging upstairs,
Door banging,
Motorbikes darting.

Heidi Burgess (9)
Langney Primary School, Eastbourne

Footy Players

Thierry Henry going through players
Being set up by a winger called Reyes.
Ronaldinho with his awesome tricks
Runs around the world as he flips and flicks.
Through his legs it's so slick
Finishes off with an overhead kick.
When Zinedine Zidane plays the defenders have to duck
Too bad he spoiled it at the end of the World Cup.
All the stars start with millions
Then they go on and make billions.

Ryan Prince (10)
Parish CE Primary School, Bromley

The Imagination Spell

A shooting star, make a wish
Mouldy cheese, stinky fish
Human nose, fin of a whale
The electricity of an eel's tail!

Spiders' silk, butterflies' wings
Ink of squid, birds that sing
Milk that's off, one sharp horn
Which could come from a unicorn.

Here is a home-made potion
Which you can use as a lotion
Drink it nicely, drink it slowly,
Sip it, slurp it, in Chemberkolli!

Evie Goss-Sampson (10)
Parish CE Primary School, Bromley

Dogs Are The Best

Dogs are special
Just the best
Better than the rest
Good companion
Brilliant friend
They will be there till the end.

Understand when you're sad,
Feeling bad
All very glad
They understand.

Dogs are special
Just the best
Better than the rest
Good companion
Brilliant friend
They will be there till the end.

Eleanor Thomas (9)
Parish CE Primary School, Bromley

Bedtime Story Time

I love my striped pyjamas,
I love my nice soft hat
My toes are warm and cosy
My slippers take care of that.
I'm washed and ready for my bed
Bang on the seventh chime
That means my clock is telling me
It's bedtime story time!

Charley O'Donnell (9)
Parish CE Primary School, Bromley

The Storm

T orrential rain plummets from the sky,
H ail also comes down with an angry force,
E veryone silently sits in their homes, praying.

S adly, everywhere is flooding,
T rees fall from great heights,
O n the beach, debris is washed-up,
R ight in front of our eyes, our town is destroyed by a monster,
M isery has come with the storm.

Rebecca Li (10)
Parish CE Primary School, Bromley

A Friendship Poem

If you ever need me,
I'll always be right here,
to chase away the sadness,
and wipe away a tear.

If you ever need me,
I'll be two steps behind,
to follow in your footsteps,
and hear what's in your mind.

If you ever need me,
you'll never have to fear,
that your presence is important,
and love is always dear.

If you ever need me,
I'll always be around,
to bring back the laughter,
that deep in your heart is found.

You'll never have to worry,
for I'll always be there,
to chase away the sadness,
and wipe away a tear.

I am here for you!

Danielle Laporte (8)
Parish CE Primary School, Bromley

Old School Friend

Based on a true story

We used to play together
Quite a lot,
But now we are split,
One of us had to go.

Alex went to Switzerland,
And I was left back home,
Now that he is out of my life,
I have no best friend.

But one day I got a call,
To invite me to his home,
I was really happy,
And couldn't wait to go.

When I got to Switzerland,
I met my old school friend,
But when it was time to go,
I thought it was the end.

A month later I got a call,
To say he was coming back,
I couldn't believe it,
My friend was coming back.

When he came back
I heard the news,
He wasn't going to be at my school,
We wouldn't see each other that much,
But it didn't matter,
I found he lived next door,
To be with him more time,
A friendship not to be torn.

Jack Zissell (10)
Parish CE Primary School, Bromley

Football

Football is a great game,
That you play in two teams.
Full of excitement and exercise.
Which each race, to win the game and fame,
But it's not all about winning
As each team tries to score a goal
It's about having fun, with your friends
And kicking the football

Score: one-nil
Some players play for a profession
Others play for fun
But either way it keeps the players on the run!

Megan Wright (9)
Parish CE Primary School, Bromley

Football

Football, football,
It's ever so great
I love it so much
I'll play out till late.

Football, football
It's been through history
Mastering all those skills
It's such a mystery.

Football, football
Made up with skill
When you're playing
You just can't stand still.

Molly Margiotta (9)
Parish CE Primary School, Bromley

The Lollipop Man

He stands by the road in the morning
And again at quarter to three
He makes us cross safely
When our parents aren't there to see.

He holds his stick like a soldier
Warning enemies that they must wait
So us children can cross over
So we are not late.

He gives us a smile
Or a friendly word or two
What can we do without him
We will all be left feeling blue.

Nilojana Nirmalan (9)
Parish CE Primary School, Bromley

The Knight

In the night,
The knight fights
The dragon that bites.

In the day,
The knight goes away
To get his horse ready for battle
To kill the knights riding the cattle.
The knight felt proud,
So he sang out loud.

Henry Miller (7)
Parish CE Primary School, Bromley

My Mummy

I love my mummy and my mummy loves me,
She makes me my dinner and my tea.

She does so much for me and my brothers,
And not to mention all the others.

And when it's time for bed
We lay down our sleepy heads,
That's where my mummy says,
'I like them sleeping best!'

Earl Theo McInnis (9)
Parish CE Primary School, Bromley

Books

Books, books everywhere,
So many to choose,
So beware!

Scary, funny, happy and sad,
Some make me laugh,
Some make me mad.

I laugh, I cry, but never walk by
A book that's saying
Come on and give me a try!

Sophie Evans (9)
Parish CE Primary School, Bromley

All My Treasures

All my treasures safe and sound
Buried in my garden ground
No one knows my secret place
The special code is safely locked in my case.
All my treasures delicate and shiny
Kept together with my keys so tiny
All my friends are so desperate to know
But I shall never tell them so.

Eliz Mullali (9)
Parish CE Primary School, Bromley

The Church Of The Living Dead

The church doors open as I walk in,
Face-to-face with the sinners of Satan.
I'm shocked and so I take a step back,
But the pathway to safety is a wall of black.

Colourless and lifeless, with no expression,
Ambling towards me like they have an obsession.
Blood dripping from their eyes,
Like bombs dropping from the skies.

They get out their swords and cut off my head,
I wake up lying in my bed.
The sinners of Satan are no longer there,
I call to my mum, 'I've had a nightmare!'

Jamie Barker (9)
Potley Hill Primary School, Yateley

Sally Cat

Black, black, black
As a night sky with no stars,
As a new tyre on the road,
As dark as my dancing trousers,
As black as my cat.

Furry, furry, furry
As a newly washed towel,
As a soft fluffy carpet,
As my brand-new slippers,
As furry as my cat.

Cuddly, cuddly, cuddly
As my favourite teddy,
As my mummy and daddy,
As a fresh plump pillow,
As cuddly as my cat.

Sally is my best friend,
She gives me lots of pleasure.
She is fun to play with,
She is my cat.

Paige Brown (10)
Potley Hill Primary School, Yateley

Heathland

Heathland, it is so rare.
I like looking at the heather and hedgehogs
I like listening to the birds singing and the crickets whistling
I like smelling the lavender
I like eating some blackberries
I like feeling the wind rustling in the long grass
Heathland, I love the heathland!

Euan O'Mahony (7)
Potley Hill Primary School, Yateley

Splodge

A speedy-shoes fur ball,
Her ears bouncing like a ball.
She is a puppy full of love,
Although she is very small.
Spotty, white and brown,
With a patch on her left eye,
A wiggle-waggle tail,
There is no way she can be shy.
Chasing her own tail,
Then racing through our home,
Chewing on my shoe,
Then eating the phone.
She's Splodge, and she's my puppy,
I love her loads and loads
She's a puppy at the moment,
But a doggie when she grows.

Ellie White (9)
Potley Hill Primary School, Yateley

My Dog Henry

Henry is a boxer
He has short brown hair
And a tail that is not there.

His wet black nose nudges me
To come and play in the garden.

Running and jumping
To catch the ball
Bring it back to me
To play some more.

When he is tired
He goes to sleep
Often, at my dad's feet.

Georgia Warner (9)
Potley Hill Primary School, Yateley

Horses

An Arab mare for Lady Jones,
Strutting around town as white as bones,
Rising in the saddle all on her own.

A shaggy shire horse was blustering Bill,
Hauling coal to the top of the hill,
Never complains but works with a will.

Old Mr Brown the chestnut hack,
Plods around with kids on his back,
Laughing and bouncing like corn in a sack.

A Shetland pony for Little Miss Sport,
A perky chappie who is ever so short,
Won't learn his lesson until he is taught.

A piebald horse for Gypsy Dover,
Looks like a jigsaw all the way over,
Chews at the grass beside the Land Rover.

Horses big, horses small,
How the owners love them all!

Emily Mackie (10)
Potley Hill Primary School, Yateley

Summertime

Summertime, rhythm and rhyme
Flowers are blooming, sun is looming
People are dozing, animals are grazing
Horses trotting, cream clotting
Waves dancing, ponies prancing
Colour shivering in the light,
Gold and silver, black and white,
All the colours of the rainbow.
That's the beauty of summertime.

Kerrie Pither (10)
Potley Hill Primary School, Yateley

My Family

My family are all nutters
They are really very strange
I know they are weird
But I hope they never change

First there's me, Charlie Jay,
Only nine with a lot to say
Then there's my little brother, little Josh,
Who gets me into all sorts of trouble

Next there's Mum, who's rather nice
And spends her time cooking smelly curry and rice
That leaves my dad, who's football mad,
Who likes to sing but it's *very* bad!

The only one that isn't strange
Is Misty, my little black cat,
She loves to sleep and eat all day
Which is why she's very fat!

Charlie Smith (9)
Potley Hill Primary School, Yateley

My Uncle Josh

My Uncle Josh is only 13,
In the war he wishes he'd been.
Guns, bombs and gas masks are his thing,
Classical music he likes to sing.
He's squishy like a cuddly bear,
He never shares but he is always fair.
He is as bright as anyone can be,
I love my uncle and he loves me.
We both look after each other,
He is like my brother.

Lauryn Lee Raymond (10)
Potley Hill Primary School, Yateley

Horse

A horse all cuddly, soft and white;
As it gallops through the night,
I get on the saddle and it feels just right,
I am lucky it does not bite.

Its fur is like a velvet cover,
Then it sees its beautiful mother,
It starts making loud sounds,
You can hear it from a faraway town.

Then they jump tall and high;
Tall enough to reach the sky,
You can hear them trotting everywhere,
People could see them in a funfair.

Then her mother leaves for a bath,
They say goodbye and then they laugh,
I brush my horse at the end of the day,
Then it gives a great big neigh.

Now she needs to go to bed,
I give her a fluffy ted,
I put a blanket over her fur,
She is happy, I am glad for her.

Emily Hourahane (9)
Potley Hill Primary School, Yateley

My Pet Tarantula

My pet tarantula is called Dum Dum
He is as black as the night
He is as hairy as a lion's mane
His legs are as long as ladders
He crawls along the floor as fast as lightning
He isn't very cuddly, but I love him so.

Jake Maxwell (7)
Potley Hill Primary School, Yateley

My Puppy, Ella Belle

Ella Belle is my puppy Westie
She is very white and very tufty
With pointy ears and a black nose
She listens wherever she goes
I love her best when she plays ball
Although she does nothing at all
I think she loves me and my sister best
Because we find her such a pest
She goes to bed with her head down low
Wishing we would never go
But the morning brings another day
Just like yesterday
I love my puppy Ella Belle
Even with that doggy smell!

Lucy Hagger (9)
Potley Hill Primary School, Yateley

My Rabbit

I have a rabbit
All soft and warm
A whiskery face on our green lawn.
He digs the grass and stamps his feet
Whenever he likes in the cold or heat.
His ears are floppy, his fur is brown
He can run fast but mostly lays down.
Where he sleeps is full of straw
There is a mesh over his front door.
He eats the plants and some brown stuff,
In the summer he loses all his fluff.

Mason Lelliott (9)
Potley Hill Primary School, Yateley

Who Is It?

There is someone special and kind to me,
Who loves to swim when we go in the sea,
Who runs and jumps and plays with her ball,
Who is brown and hairy but not very tall.

She has four legs and tiny paws,
And uses her nose to open the doors,
She plays with her toys and jumps at the boys,
On firework night she hates the noise!

She has big, floppy, dangly ears,
She's lived with us now for nearly three years,
She's happy and friendly and really good fun,
I usually stroke her when football is done!

She sits and waits for me to come home,
And when she is good I give her a bone,
She shows me the way when I'm lost in the fog,
Her name is Jess and she is my dog!

Shaun Sims (11)
Potley Hill Primary School, Yateley

My Cat Smudge

I have a black and white cat
Who eats loads and he is very fat

He loves playing with his toy mouse
But he can't get through the flap to the house

Smudge rarely gets into fights
And he doesn't go upstairs because he is afraid of heights

He occasionally is a big wuss
Although he can be an aggressive little puss

Smudge sounds active but he is actually lazy
Although he can get really crazy

He is a British Shorthair
And we give him loads of care

Charlotte Forshaw (9)
Potley Hill Primary School, Yateley

Football Poem

My name is Christian and I score lots of goals
I play in a team called Potley and Frogmore FC
Our team is under 11's and we are in division one
Last week we played away and we won 4-1
Playing up front is what I like best
Running up the field away from the rest.

We train every week on a Thursday night
Now it's winter it's not very light
Passing and shooting is what we do
Corners, crossing and jogging too.

Football is my favourite sport
Manchester United is the team I support
Watching or playing I like it all
But best of all is kicking a ball.

Christian Barrett (10)
Potley Hill Primary School, Yateley

Yoda

Yoda, Yoda, Yoda the Jedi,
Yoda will fight and has yet to die,

Yoda is an alien and comes from Star Wars,
And you will never find him in a game called car wars,
Yoda is good at fighting and very small,
He has a green face that is very cool,

Yoda has the force,
And sometimes can go of course

Yoda, Yoda, he has a green lightsaber,
And the sort of thing he would say would be,
'Don't save me, save her'.

Yoda, Yoda speaks like a human,
And wouldn't give in at the point of a gun.

Christopher Bates (9)
Potley Hill Primary School, Yateley

My Dog Connie

My dog has yellow, furry, fluffy hair,
Her legs aren't as stable as a chair.

She has a brown collar made of leather
And her nails are like the point of a feather.

She doesn't like the sound of breaking glass,
And when the glass men come she runs off as quick as a blast.

She sleeps in the kitchen sometimes
And she loves it when the sun shines.

When we come home from school
Connie just wants to jump into the pool.

She wants to play just like a puppy
Which makes me feel sad,
When I think of all the good times we have had.

You see Connie is nearly 14
And that would make 98 in our years
I will always love and remember
My lovely dog called Connie.

Ben Cook (10)
Potley Hill Primary School, Yateley

My Rabbit

Hi, my name is Fudge.
I am brown and hop around.
I have long floppy ears that hang to the ground
My teeth are long and sparkly white,
They love to munch on all things bright.
My nose twitches all the time,
Sniffing everything that I find.
My eyes open wide when you appear,
Knowing it's feeding time.
Loving all the attention that I get,
I finally lay down upon my hay.

Sophie Langdon (9)
Potley Hill Primary School, Yateley

Lego Star Wars

L is for Lego, the creator of the game
E is for exciting, the thrill of the game
G is the great, the wonderful game play
O is for opportunities, there is so much in the game

S is for secrets, about the game
T is for tournament, there are a few challenges
A is for alternate, you can read keep the trilogy or change it
R is for riding, you can ride different vehicles

W is for war, the game is about a Star Wars' battle
A is for achieve, you can accomplish loads of things
R is for reading, you read to understand the levels
S is for special, there are hidden power bricks

2 is for 2, it is the second game in the sequel.

Lewis Rosier (10)
Potley Hill Primary School, Yateley

A World

A world with fun, it can weigh a ton.
A world with toys, just for boys.
A world with sweets, not meat.
A world with trees, filled with bees.
A world with food, that puts me in a good mood.
A world with Coke, not smoke.
A world with games on the River Thames.
A world with books, tied on hooks.
A world with school, just not cool.
A world with flowers, on towers.
A great world, a nice world, that's all I want!

Jackson Bailey (9)
Potley Hill Primary School, Yateley

Seasons

Spring is here at last
New buds are budding
Bright yellow daffodils growing tall and fast
Baby lambs skipping happily
Days are getting longer
Goodbye winter nights.

Hot, hot, sunny summer days
Glistening golden sand shimmering in the sun
Brilliant bright blue seas
Children having lots of fun
Sandcastles big and small
Ice cream cold and yummy

It is autumn now, gone is the heat
The leaves have changed colours
Hallowe'en; trick or treat
Everyone together eating sweets
Catherine wheels whizzing round
Rockets going up leaving shooting stars behind.

Cold grey winter has come
Ho, ho, ho Santa is here
So turn on the Christmas lights at home
And open your presents now.
Children are making snowmen
Having fun playing in the snow.

Lucy Allen (10)
Potley Hill Primary School, Yateley

The Busy Circus

Music deafening.
Crowds gathering.
Tickets shown.
Seat picked.
I wait.
Show begins.

Horses canter.
Elephants trumpet.
Seals bark.
Tigers roar.
Granny laughs.
Monkeys shriek.

Trapeze swings.
Strongman lifts.
Tightrope walks.
Acrobats flip.
Mum's thrilled.
Magician tricks.

Finale flies.
Acts bow.
Crowd thins.
Ringmaster drones.
Dad snores.
Seats empty.

We walk.
We laugh.
We share.
We talk.
We relax.
We enjoyed.

Josh Morgan (10)
Potley Hill Primary School, Yateley

My Family

My name is Sam and I am 10 years old,
I live in a house that we have just recently sold.

I have two younger brothers that drive me insane,
They are cheeky and Charlie, these are their names.

My mum is very beautiful with lovely long hair,
I will never find another mum because she's very rare.

My daddy is very tall and lots and lots of fun,
He's happy and he's jolly, he's like a ray of sun.

We just bought a cat, he is white from head to toe,
And in the cold wintertime you could lose him in the snow.

I've now come to the end, I've nothing more to say,
Except I hope you like my poem as I wrote it in a day.

Samuel Morgan (10)
Potley Hill Primary School, Yateley

Who Am I?

I live in the grass
Lots of things pass
I jump so high
But I can't fly
I am purple and green
I'm hardly seen
I am so small
The grass is so tall
I make noises at night
That give people a fright
Can you guess who I am?

A: Grasshopper.

Courtney Chiles (9)
Potley Hill Primary School, Yateley

A Tree

A tree
is green and brown.
Every year the leaves grow then fall.
It is a home to robins, magpies, crows,
blackbirds, squirrels, doves and sparrows.
In autumn the leaves turn yellow, brown
and golden red and start to fall.
The wind blows the leaves and they flutter
everywhere like children in a playground.
In winter the leaves curl up and die and
the tree is bare and lonely.
In spring the buds
grow back
and the
tree is
green again.

Charlotte Heape (8)
Potley Hill Primary School, Yateley

Life As An Ant

I am an ant and I live in the grass
I have short legs and move quite fast.
I carry food on my back
Which I eat as a snack.
We live in a hole
That's as black as a mole.

I have lots of sisters and brothers
And only one mother.
We sometimes climb tall trees
And meet other ants and buzzing bees.
We work very hard day by day
We all come home and then we play.

Liam Morgan (7)
Potley Hill Primary School, Yateley

Butterfly

Butterfly, butterfly, flying through the sunny sky as the clouds go by
Ever busy looking for nectar
Marigold, daisy, rose or clover
What today is your delight?
Maybe a feast, primrose or violet
Oh, butterfly, butterfly, flying through the sunny sky.

Butterfly, butterfly, flying through the meadow oh so bright
Tall grass swaying in the breeze
Watch out it might make you
Sneeze!
Butterfly, butterfly, flying away
Bye, bye butterfly, bye-bye.

Isabella Hart (8)
Potley Hill Primary School, Yateley

The Cricket Match

Wooden bat, missing ball
Thud of wicket hitting ground
Happy bowler standing proud
Shouting fans, sirens loud

Batter smashing ball for six
Bowler holding head in hands
Umpire holding arms to sky
England fans now jumping high

Game is over, England winners
Exhausted players in the shower
Happy fans now wait for next train
Ground is silent till the next game.

Jake Green (10)
Potley Hill Primary School, Yateley

The Web

The spider stared around the room
Until he saw a fly
He watched and watched him fly
Around and around
Until he flew into his web

He slowly watched and watched
So slowly that you could not
Ever see him move
Until he jumped on the fly
And he was alive no more.

Natasha Saunders (7)
Potley Hill Primary School, Yateley

The Creature

The door opens
I look in surprise
Pad, pad, pad
Pad, pad, pad
As it walks up to me
Its glowing eyes in the dark
Is all I see
Making a noise
Like a distant helicopter
Pad, pad, pad
Pad, pad, pad
Coming closer
Pressing against my ankles
Soft and silky
Purr, purr, purr
Purr, purr, purr
The furry creature
Is my cat.

William Wallace (9)
Potley Hill Primary School, Yateley

Wetherell Is Our Name

My name is Charlotte
I am nine
I live in Frogmore and it's divine.

I have loads of friends
Who love to play
And if I had my way
We would all stay out all day.

I have a brother
He is called Matt
But I would rather
He had been a cat.

I have a lovely mum and dad
Who love to have fun
And are really mad.

I have two dogs
Called Harley and Millie
And when they play
They are really silly.

This is my family
Wetherell is our name
And no matter what
I love them all the same.

*But I would rather have
A cat than Matt.*

Charlotte Wetherell (9)
Potley Hill Primary School, Yateley

Football Poem

M y favourite game is football,
A nd Man U is the best.
N umber eight is Wayne Rooney,
C oming with them to win the league.
H eading the balls into the goals,
E xactly like Eric Cantona.
S ilvestra is defending the ball,
T o make sure they don't score.
E ven in the hardest games,
R ooney scores the most.

U nder Alex Ferguson's formation,
N o one can do better.
I n matches it's a rough battle,
T ogether we will win.
E nd of the league and we have got the cup,
D efending all our matches.

F ootball will always be the best,
O ther sports can't beat it.
O nly footie beats the rest.
T he fans of Man U are across the world,
B ecause we are the greatest.
A t Old Trafford we are kings,
L ooking at our red devil.
L etting the others know we are coming.

C lubs had better be worrying.
L ook out Chelsea, Arsenal too,
U nless you are lucky we will beat you.
B est in the world is Man U!

Colin Steer (9)
Potley Hill Primary School, Yateley

The Piano

Learning the piano is fun,
But sometimes it makes you feel glum,
You should practise each day,
Then your teacher will say,
'That's all for now. . . off you run.'

Learning the piano is tough,
And often the music sounds rough,
You should practise each day,
Then your teacher will say,
'OK Claire . . . that's enough.'

Learning the piano is fulfilling,
Taking up time, if you're willing,
You should practise each day,
Then your teacher will say,
'Music like that's worth a shilling.'

Learning the piano is fun,
But sometimes it makes you feel glum,
You should practise each day,
Then your teacher will say,
'That's very good Claire . . . well done.'

Claire Edwards (9)
Potley Hill Primary School, Yateley

World War II

Hitler is coming
Bombs dropping
Sirens wailing
People shouting, running and screaming,
Down into the shelters, with family
And neighbours
Waiting for the siren to stop wailing.
Mums and dads shouting for them to
Switch off the light!

Maddie Andrews (10)
Potley Hill Primary School, Yateley

Seasons

Spring

Fresh-cut grass
Sunshine day,
Flower smells
Newborn day.

Lambs bleating
Chicks cheeping,
Daffodils showing
No more snowing.

Summer

Apples growing
Dad's mowing,
Mum's baking bread
Flower beds.

Sun's rays
Golden hay,
Smell of barbecues
Happy days.

Autumn

Birds cheeping
Mum's sweeping,
Leaves golden-brown
Falling down.

Bonfire smells
And chestnuts shells,
Leaves crunchy
Harvests munchies.

Winter

Crackling fires
Crunchy snow,
Mornings misty
Winds gusty
Berries red
Warm bed.

Alicia Dallibar
Potley Hill Primary School, Yateley

Ronie, My Furry Friend

Ronie is a furry dog who likes hunting for frogs.
She doesn't eat them, she follows them around,
The garden while sniffing them.

She loves going down to our boat
And barks at all the swans,
The swans tease her by hissing at her.

She swims like a fish and when she emerges from the water
She looks like a drowned rat.
She shakes vigorously and makes me wet.

I love her very much,
We play together and she makes me laugh
So much that I cry.

Amy Herbert (9)
Potley Hill Primary School, Yateley

Football

Football, football, football
The season is here again
Running, training, kicking
Getting fit again
Up and down the pitch we run
It can be so much fun
It's nice to be a winning team
And helps you let off steam

The manager stands on the
Touchline screaming,
Pass the ball, I hear a shout
With the wind in my hair
I kicked the ball in the air
It's in the net, the whistle blows
Football, football time is now at an end.

George Goodsell (10)
Potley Hill Primary School, Yateley

The Diamond Shop

This is the safe with an iron base
That holds the code to the diamond shop.
This is the beam that lets off poisonous steam
Around the safe with the iron base
That holds the code to the diamond shop.
This is the guard with the card
That turns off the beam that lets off poisonous steam
Around the safe with the iron base
That holds the code to the diamond shop.
This is the robber with an AK-47
Which can send people to Heaven
Which he did to the guard then took the card
And shut off the beam that lets off poisonous steam
Went to the safe with the iron base
And took the code to the diamond shop.
These are the police that caught the robber
Who'd done a terrible crime
And went to jail for a lifetime.

Jason Allen (9)
Potley Hill Primary School, Yateley

The Grey Ghost

A grey spectre poised on a misty meadow.
An illusion of molten silver blending into the fog.
Two golden eyes pierce the smoky haze.
It's the grey ghost called the Weimeraner.
He is cloaked in mystery, power and endurance.
His devotion and loyalty only to his master and family.
The grey ghost is highly intelligent and affectionate.
He's fearless and protective and will track and retrieve.
He is bold and assertive and will bark to alert of strangers.
That is the grey ghost called the Weimeraner.

Connor Maxted (10)
Potley Hill Primary School, Yateley

My Holiday

Hooray, it's time for us to pack our case,
shorts and T-shirts all rolled up tight,
all ready for us to take our flight.
Golden sands and sparkling sea,
waiting at the beach just for me,
to swim and splash,
with waves so big
now it's time to make a dash.

The waves were rolling in,
white and high, we saw a jet ski,
but it was much too fast for me.
On the sand, a pedal boat I spied,
'Come on Dad', I cried.
Mum and Dad and sister too,
pedalled out into the sea so blue.

Brother Jamie looking happy,
playing in the golden sand with Nanny.
Then off we go to find our pool,
I dived in and out, oh so cool.

Our holiday has come to an end,
no more money for me to spend.
A happy time we all have had,
no, I must not be feeling sad.

Thomas Smallbone (10)
Potley Hill Primary School, Yateley

Terrifying Noises

As I heard the siren, I knew what I had to do.
We went under the table and put a gas mask on.
My friend was terrified and I was too.

Even now I had the gas mask on
I could not see anything far away
I could only see things near me
Because of the fumes from the bomb.
The only person I could see was my friend,
His name was Dom.

All this smoke around me made me want to be sick
But I couldn't be whilst in the gas mask.
The only thing I wanted to do was to get out of this mess
That was my task.
I felt like I was going to die
All the bombs going off so near me.
I wanted to go home
And have a nice cup of tea.

I wanted to relax and go to sleep but I couldn't
It was too nerve-racking to go to sleep.
And then the siren went off again
Telling us it was all over
And the last thing I remembered was Dom calling to me
Then I collapsed, passed out into a heap on the floor.

Benjamin Halvey (10)
Potley Hill Primary School, Yateley

My Friend Blu

My friend Blu is a nice little girl,
She plays with me all the time,
When she gets a little bored,
She sings a wonderful rhyme.

Her long, silky, brown hair,
Her beautiful sea-blue eyes,
Her short, smooth, grey skirt
She will always get the guys!

We love to dance together,
We are quite good at it,
Blu loves to sing a lot
But I only like it a bit.

We both like acting very much,
We think it is great fun,
When I played Loopy in Snow White,
They made me look like a ton.

So this is all about Blu
Who she is and what she likes to do
Maybe one day you might meet her
And you might like her too!

Bethany Rosier (10)
Potley Hill Primary School, Yateley

My Dog Poppy

I've just got a little puppy,
We decided to call her Poppy.
She's black with white feet,
And she's very, very sweet.
She wears a red collar,
And she is worth more than a dollar.
She likes long walks,
She is so clever she almost talks.
Poppy has long legs and runs very fast,
If she was in a race she wouldn't be last.
Her eyes are brown,
And she always frowns.
I hold her tight,
And she always wants a fight.
When I walk in the door,
She falls on the floor.
She always wags her tail,
And it never fails.
She likes to sleep on my bed,
She is good company.
I love her very much and she loves me.

Summer French (10)
Potley Hill Primary School, Yateley

Friends

Friends are much more fun to have,
Than just your brother, mum and dad.
I can do different things with my friends every day,
Football and swimming and lots of play,
Game Boy and PlayStation and piano too,
We can do anything we want to do.

Summer holidays are best of all,
Without school we can have a ball.
The sun is hot and the water is cool,
It's a lot of fun not being in school.
At school we have to work all day,
Apart from break when we get to play.

At my house we do it all,
Including parties and football.
Sleepovers are best of all,
Especially when we watch Liverpool.

At Christmas we have presents
And we share one and all.
So friends are the best of all
Be kind to them or you will lose them all.

Jordan Lambert (9)
Potley Hill Primary School, Yateley

Cricket

Cricket is a sport,
Cricket is fun,
One over,
Six balls,
Hit boundaries down the ground,
Hit sixes out of the ground,
No ball,
No call,
Wrong call,
You're out!
Half century,
Century!
Pro 40 to one a day,
The best is the 20/20,
England V Australia, The Ashes,
The biggest game of them all,
Very nerve-racking!
Competitive but fun,
I have only just begun,
One day I hope to be . . .
The next Freddie Flintoff!

Harry Bowman (10)
Potley Hill Primary School, Yateley

Food

Some food is healthy
Some food is yummy
Most of the food is
Cooked by your mummy

Cakes are scrummy
So are these
Potatoes, carrots,
Ice cream and cheese.

Fish is yuck
So are these
Beef, lamb and
Pepper makes you sneeze

We have lots of food
So we should be grateful
Some countries aren't so lucky
So we shouldn't waste a mouthful.

Ellen Pearce (9)
Potley Hill Primary School, Yateley

George

George was a spider,
Who lived in my bath.
He was black and hairy,
My mum thinks he was scary.
He ran up the walls,
And climbed up the taps.
When he was hungry,
He ate up the flies.

Where did he go?
I don't know!

Callum Chappell (8)
Potley Hill Primary School, Yateley

My Dog Gus

Gus is my pet, he has blonde, black and brown hair.
He is an Alsation that likes to play ball.
People think that he is scary, he looks scary, he barks really loud,
But he never bites, he is scared of little dogs and baths.
I le is really soft and very soft inside. He loves bones.
If he's done something wrong his ears will flap down
And his eyes will look up at you.
He will go hyper if you say *walkies, bone, stick, biscuit* or if you fight.
He wears a silver collar that jangles when he walks.
He has his own brush that keeps his fur tidy
And he has his own bowl that he drinks and eats out of.

Nathan Connolly (10)
Potley Hill Primary School, Yateley

Dragons

Dragons are smart and very helpful
They help you with anything,
When you need a hand.

My mother used to tell me that dragons
Don't exist, but I know better.
So now I am sitting here, my dragon
Here beside me helping me with my poem.

Dragons come in different colours,
They may be sparkly green,
Might be red or blue or shimmering silver,
Mine is a gold called Queen.

Some people think that dragons
Are just a child's imagination,
But I know you won't, because,
Dragons are smart and very helpful.

Siân Wells (10)
Potley Hill Primary School, Yateley

Homework

Homework, oh homework, oh how I love homework
Sometimes it is easy and sometimes pretty hard
But I will still do it so that I can learn

You have to read and write in English,
Sometimes it is easy and sometimes pretty hard

We learnt about the past and present in history
Again, sometimes it is easy and sometimes pretty hard

In maths it is sums and problems
Again, sometimes it is easy and sometimes pretty hard

Homework, oh homework, oh how I love homework.

Danielle Moir (9)
Potley Hill Primary School, Yateley

The Monster

Underneath the floorboards
In the shadows there is a monster
It groans and mumbles all-night
And wakes up the baby,
It creeps along your bed at midnight
And into your dreams,
It steals your comics
And breaks the electronics.
At dinner it burps
And makes more rude noises,
And you get sent to your room,
And you're made to eat leftovers.
It sends slugs and spiders up the toilet
When you're on the loo,
And tears up your newspaper and eats it.
But its favourite thing is to . . .
Eat people.

Alex Pritchard (10)
Potley Hill Primary School, Yateley

Santa Claus

Icy frost, white and cold, covered the grass
As eleven fifty-nine turned to twelve o'clock,
He started his journey, soaring, flying, his sleigh approached.

Presents, presents filled his sleigh with amazing colours.
He landed on glittering white roofs.
And delivered the beautifully wrapped presents to the awaiting trees.

More dazzling snow fell to the ground laying white blankets.
He returned to his cold, snowy home, just as it turned six thirty.
Smiles and laughter waited for children.

Thomas Kent (10)
Potley Hill Primary School, Yateley

One Day At The Zoo

One day I went to the zoo
I took my friend Maria too
We saw lions, tigers, giraffes and bears
All under the zoo's care

Then we went to see some shows with
Dolphins and whales
And the whales had huge tails
They made a big splash
So we had to dash
We hid behind the keeper's hut
Then played pitch and putt

Lunch was next
And I sent a text
To my mum, saying we're having fun
The weather was great
But getting late
So we had to go through the iron gate.

Lucy Rampling (9)
Potley Hill Primary School, Yateley

New York

Pass beneath Brooklyn's dusky arch,
Many people on the march.
Thick grey cables made of steel
Staying on an even keel.

Clickety-clack echoes around,
Decoration everywhere, it will astound.
Silver and bronze cover the clock
Hands moving steadily, *tick-tock, tick-tock*.

Like asparagus soaring high in the sky,
Its spirit will never die.
One hundred and two floors to the top
It seems that it will never stop.

Massive copper sheets make up the lady,
She rules Manhattan, turquoise and shady.
Strong Liberty and powerful
She sends a message to us all.

Colourful advertising screens,
Wonderful objects of people's dreams.
Crossroads of the world, they say
Running to and fro all the day.

Nathanael King (10)
Potley Hill Primary School, Yateley

My Holiday

Time to wake up, it's Sunday today,
The time has come to go on holiday.
Wales today is our destination,
It's a long drive through our nation.

After three hours drive we are finally here,
My dad's gone straight off to find himself a beer.
The keeper's taken us to find our chalet,
It was the best one, luckily we came today.

A couple of days later it's time to go to the beach,
But with a difference, the sky isn't peach.
I hold my skim board as I walk to the sea,
And I find myself being attacked by a bee!
But I don't care because I am too excited,
And that's when everything gets exaggerated.

Today was the best ever,
That was the record to be beaten never.

Now the holiday has come to an end,
This place will be my forever friend.

Liam Cox (9)
Potley Hill Primary School, Yateley

The Grassland

Long green grass blowing in the wind
On a hot sunny day
Busy bees buzzing from one flower to another
Grasshoppers happily hopping in the grass
Daddy-long-legs flying in the breeze
Spiders spinning their silky webs
Pink heather hiding a skylark's nest.

Yellow buttercups blowing in the wind
Dogs barking and running around
The owners calling their dogs to fetch a stick
Children playing catch with a bright yellow ball
Nibbling rabbits eating the grass
Hopping off into their burrows
All these things I see when I'm wandering around the grassland.

Laurel Glazier (7)
Potley Hill Primary School, Yateley

Bike

My bike is a BMX,
Red, silver and black.
Feel happy on my bike,
I enjoy it and it's fun.
I feel good and free from homework.

Sometimes my trousers get caught in the chain,
Then I lose control of my bike.
I'm the fastest in my road,
And the only BMX rider, I still win.

When I go fast it feels like my
Head is out of the car window,
Thrilling and exciting.
My bike is a BMX.

Harry Butler (10)
Potley Hill Primary School, Yateley

Weather

Oh how I love to be out in the air
To live and breathe it everywhere,
I love the wind with its swelling and hurling sound,
Its cool breeze blowing through my hair
And that gentle whistle everywhere.

In the sun I like the warm air with flowers growing
And blowing in the breeze and the bees buzzing all around.
And how I like the rain for splashing and jumping in puddles,
And without the rain we would have no life.

Last of all I love the snow, the snow makes me happy
I love to be out in the snow, playing and jumping
Cold, wet eyes, makes my face and hands cold
Which makes me laugh and giggle.

Paige Calcott (9)
Potley Hill Primary School, Yateley

Pets

There are tall ones, thin ones, short ones and fat ones.
Some can jump and some can climb.
Some can run and some can hide.
Some are cute and some are cuddly.
Some can be dangerous too.

Some are friendly, some are mean
Few do tricks and few do none
Some can swing from tree to tree and even follow you around,
Some are fun to play with and some are not at all.
Some have long beaks and some have none at all.

Fur, feathers, scales or skin,
Black, white, red or green,
No matter what their colour or kind,
Pets are loved the whole world wide.

Victoria Herridge (9)
Potley Hill Primary School, Yateley

The Seaside

The sand slid straight through my toes and buried my feet.
While the sun's beams hit me with a blasting wave of heat.
The ocean softly kisses the shore and the smooth
and slippery pebbles while the fish below swim freely and happily
through the coral beds and seaweed.

You could smell the shop's ice cream from a mile away,
with its sweet, watery and creamy centre, as well as the strong drinks
and freshly made doughnuts.
The seagulls swooped down to the ground collecting small fish
by the shore or even the leftovers that people have dropped,
greedily wanting more.

The shouting of people filled the air, playing beach
and water games like volleyball and surfing and many more.
Colours everywhere, like the last glimpse of the sun reflecting
off the ocean like they will never meet again.
Blue and white striped deckchairs being packed away
and put in the cars, leaving the beach.

Anthony Slocombe (10)
Potley Hill Primary School, Yateley

Crazy Creatures

This bird is strange, it barked at me.
It's probably a budgie, blue and brown it's easy to see.
It made its footprint on the ground
These strange animals are easy to be found.

What a strange frog I just saw
It had a bright green face and a fluffy paw.
He was on a lily pad eating a carrot,
He talked so much he sounded like a parrot.

Then out of the woods popped what I thought was a cat
It hooted like an owl but looked like a bat.
It was brown and fluffy with a big black wing
It screeched and fluttered over everything.

These crazy creatures are everywhere around
Up in the air and down on the ground
Some are nasty, most are kind,
But really you know they are just in your mind.

Paris O'Keeffe (9)
Potley Hill Primary School, Yateley

The Alphabet Song

A is for alligator, snapping its vicious teeth.
B is for bottle-nosed dolphin singing under the sea.
C is for cat catching a mouse.
D is for dragonfly hovering just above water.
E is for elephant squirting water everywhere.
F is for flamingo standing on one leg.
G is for gull squawking overhead.
H is for hippopotamus chewing up its food.
I is for iguana dancing around in the sun.
J is for jackdaw jumping around old abandoned places.
K is the komodo dragon eating its new carrion.
L is for leopard running extremely fast.
M is for mammoth stomping around and waving its tusks.
N is for narwhal cleverly navigating the rock formations.
O is for orang-utan swinging from tree to tree.
P is for parrot repeating everything you say.
Q is the quail quaking in the bush.
R is for a rhinoceros waving his sharp pointed horn.
S is for snake eating massive prey.
T is tarantula biting whatever it can find.
U is for ugly bugs creeping and crawling.
V is for vulture picking on bones.
W is for wolf prowling around in its pack.
X is for extraordinary animals in our imagination.
Y is for yak waving its long hair around.
Z is for zebra playing on the plain.

Alex Richman (9)
Potley Hill Primary School, Yateley

Menorca

My first time abroad in Menorca I could tell it was going to be great,
We were on the road for four hours by this rate,
I could tell we were going to be late.

My first time abroad in Menorca I could tell it was going to be great,
The flight was really cool,
But not as great as the pool.

My first time abroad in Menorca I could tell it was going to be great,
At first the pool was freezing,
But then I got my knees in.

My first time abroad in Menorca I could tell it was going to be great,
Sitting by the pool,
My sister thought she was cool.

My first time abroad in Menorca I could tell it was going to be great,
Sipping cola in the sun,
I knew it would be kind of fun.

My first time abroad in Menorca I could tell it was going to be great,
Running on the beach,
For as long as I could reach.

My first time abroad in Menorca I could tell it was going to be great,
Flying back by night,
The lights in Paris were bright.

Jade Maxwell (10)
Potley Hill Primary School, Yateley

Fairies Of The Night

F ireflies deep in the woods
A sudden glow
I n the night
R oaming in the air
I n the night sky bright
E asily
S potted

Fairies of the night.

F un and cheerful
A wing so bright
I n the luminous dark
R ed sparkles forming
I n the night sky bright
E agerly
S ilent

Fairies of the night.

Pratisha Bantawa (9)
Potley Hill Primary School, Yateley

Weather

The cold weather makes me shiver
the wind like a frosty bite
the clouds of black
everyone wrapped up warm
what a miserable day.

The stormy weather makes me quiver
everything waving around
lightning forks lighten the sky
no one is out
what a gloomy day.

The sunny weather, everyone is out
nothing stopping us playing about
look how bright the sun shines
everyone's merry and gay.

Bethan Williams (10)
Potley Hill Primary School, Yateley

Darth Vader's Rap

Yo, I'm Darth Vader
And this is my rap!
Hey, it may be weird
But just talk to the cap.

I'm feared all over the galaxy
And Skywalker is my enemy.
Solo, the Wookie and Leia too
C3PO and R2D2

When my saber's out
I have no doubt,
That you will die
And I'll eat pie.

I have the force
So you can't fool me.
In a disguise
Like the suit on me

Hey, I'm Darth Vader
And that was my rap.
So I'll see ya soon
And I'll sign ya cap!

Calum O'Mahony (9)
Potley Hill Primary School, Yateley

My Dog Henry

My dog Henry
He really does stink,
He drinks out of the toilet,
Does he ever think?

My dog Henry,
He barks all day,
He sits by the front door
Thinking, *will the post ever come today?*

My dog Henry,
He is really thick,
When he eats
He makes you feel sick.

My dog Henry,
Steals things from the table,
Sometimes he is thinking,
I wish I had read the label.

My dog Henry,
Is unique in every way,
He may be a greedy little soul
But he is my greedy dog every single day!

Laura Drake (10)
Potley Hill Primary School, Yateley

Always Watching

Always watching, waiting and hoping
Always teaching, coping
Always listening, learning and sharing
Always being there, ever caring

Sometimes scared, feared and worried
Sometimes searching, stressed, hurried
Sometimes trying, tired, and worn
Sometimes feeling all forlorn

Mostly joyful, jaunty and fine
Mostly fantastic, fun and divine
Mostly rapturous, rewarding and great
Mostly enjoying, sharing the loving

Such great loving and joy
Such letting people, girl or boy
Such a joy to help the new life
Such an honour to be the oldest.

Mary Okunsanwo ((8)
St Fidelis Catholic School, Erith

The Stars

The stars twinkle high in the sky,
The stars shine like diamonds way up high,
Oh how much prettier could they be?
The stars stare brightly at me,
Oh how much the stars twinkle with glee,
Oh how much prettier could they be?
The stars shimmer in the dark black sea,
The night sky passes by me,
Oh how much prettier could they be?

Rachel Brown (9)
St Fidelis Catholic School, Erith

My Alien Dream

I have a little alien and he comes from outer space,
He is very green and slimy and he has a funny face.
We play and play the whole night long, he loves to watch TV,
We have the best time ever, he's the best friend there could be.
In the morning, when the sun comes out, my friend, Slimy has to go,
But he'll be back again tonight, to play our games, I know.

Shhhh, shhhh!

Phoebe O'Reilly (7)
St Fidelis Catholic School, Erith

School Kidz

Hey my name is Isobel
I've got to run,
Today's the day
I have fun

I'm a popular kid
Look at me,
Art is my thing
As you can see.

I'm very hungry
Let's grab our lunch,
Let's have it you
Let's have a chew
And one big munch.

It's the end of the day
I've had a great laugh,
It's time to go home
And have a hot bath.

Isobel Pinto (10)
St Fidelis Catholic School, Erith

Groovy Granddad

He may be getting old
But he can do the jig,
And he's not very bald
So he doesn't need a wig.

When we're at the water park
He goes on all the slides!
Also at Chessington
He went on all the rides!

He likes watching football
And telling funny jokes,
He tells them to all
Different kinds of folks.

He's my groovy granddad
And I love him so,
And my groovy grandma
As well, you know!

Chloe Huggon (8)
St Fidelis Catholic School, Erith

The Candle Flame

The candle flame is shining bright,
Like a butterfly fluttering by.
The candle flame dances like a swan
By the river by the pond.
The candle flame is the dancing star
It lights up the blue sky,
The candle flame never stops dancing
In the dark night.
It dances like a dancing fairy.

Melanie Andrade (9)
St Fidelis Catholic School, Erith

My Budgie Called Smokey

I had a bird called Smokey Bacon
He was always cheerful and happy
He thought he was pretty
How wonderful is that?
He always looked at himself in the mirror and said, 'I'm a pretty boy.'

One day he followed my mum out the door
He flew away so we got another one called Minty
I saw Smokey, sad, looking at Jack play with Minty
Smokey had come back to play.

Faye Larkins (8)
St Fidelis Catholic School, Erith

School Dinners

School dinners are yuck
Just like muck
Don't you agree with me?

Like your food
Do not get in a mood
Please don't shout
Just eat your sprout

Why do you disagree?
Because I am me
I never agree with anything

Don't think you are great
You're not even my mate
Don't slurp your plate
OK?

Zarah Pinto (8)
St Fidelis Catholic School, Erith

Enduring Love

God's love is devoted,
His love blossoms like the evergreen flower.
God's love radiates the whole entire world,
With His loving beams He will cleanse each and every one of us.

God's compassion and tenderness,
Makes me think about Him every day.
When I gaze above me I can feel,
God protecting me.

God is tranquil,
He is very dear-hearted.
God lets us be free,
But tends to us every now and again.

We should abide in God's shelter,
And God's loving beams will cleanse the world.

Omoye Osebor (10)
St Fidelis Catholic School, Erith

My Dream

Is there something in my room,
Or is it just the shadow of the moon?
I'm very, very scared,
What shall I do?
Do not worry,
Do not be in a hurry,
Go to sleep,
And forget all those horrible dreams.
But I still can't get to sleep,
So I'll try counting sheep,
But I still can't get to sleep,
So I'll bury my head under my sheet,
And hope very soon I'll be fast asleep.

Marianne Jennings (7)
St Fidelis Catholic School, Erith

Flowers

All flowers are beautiful in their own special way.
I like roses the best because I saw one today.
The rose that I saw was lovely and pink,
But I also like red ones, I think.
What about daffodils and foxgloves and lillies,
I think they are pretty as well.
I would probably also stop and look at the bluebell.
All these lovely colours make me feel happy today.
So I'll keep on looking for flowers on my way.

Cristina Buscaglia (7)
St Fidelis Catholic School, Erith

What Am I

I am a tabby,
But well-groomed.

I am happy,
But I am stern.

I am a toy,
But not very playful.

What am I?

I look light,
But I am very heavy.

I am a jump,
But not spring.

I have hair,
But not little.

What am I?

I am a . . . *cat.*

Catherine Melder (10)
St Fidelis Catholic School, Erith

My Day

One day when I was walking down the street,
A gust of wind lifted me off my feet,
It swirled me around and took me up high,
Where I found a yellow door hanging in the sky,
I opened the door and looked inside,
And I found a wonderful garden to my surprise.
That opened my eyes
To see the fantastic flowers inside,
There were lots of trees inside there, which were floating in the air,
My feet suddenly touched the ground with a thud!
And that was my brilliant day!

Rebecca Wheatley (8)
St Fidelis Catholic School, Erith

Animals

Some are big
And some are small,
Some are short
And some are tall.

Some miaow
And some bark,
Some are pets
And like the park.

Some live in zoos
And are given their food,
Others go hunting
If they're in the mood.

I like all the animals
Both in zoos and in farms,
They are all very different
And all have different charms.

Tanya Nour (9)
St Fidelis Catholic School, Erith

Seasons All Over

Springtime comes around each year,
Bringing warmth and lots of cheer.
Daffodils and daisies start to appear,
At last we know that spring is here.

Summer days come round at last,
Now is the time to cut the grass.
We need to dig, to plant apple seeds,
So our gardens grow like weeds.

The autumn leaves have all turned brown,
They die and twirl to the ground.
The branches there, all dark and bare,
No longer can birds shelter there.

The winter ground dresses in white,
The brilliant sun reflects the light.
The beautiful snow begins to fall,
As branches sway, big and small.

Charlotte Rootsey (9)
St Fidelis Catholic School, Erith

War and Peace

Peace
Peace is as white as angels
It smells as pure as red poppies
Peace tastes of the bread and wine of Passover
It sounds like the shouts of joy
It feels like Heaven touching the Earth
Peace lives everywhere and brings happiness and hope.

War
War is as red as blood
It is the smell of gunpowder
War tastes of the soil stained with blood
It sounds like howling war cries
It feels like a sword slicing you open
War lives in everything bad and waits for combat.

Thomas Rawlings (10)
St Fidelis Catholic School, Erith

Dreams

Dreams are what everyone has,
Dreams are the future we are coming up to.
Dreams are made at home in your comfortable bed,
Dreams are also made at school,
Your imagination goes wild when you write a story about your dreams.
Why can't the world be like a dream? I wonder
Dreams will always come true.
So what you dream will come true if you believe in it.

Hannah Akinshade (9)
St Fidelis Catholic School, Erith

The Hungry Man

I was walking in the sun
trying to have some fun
and saw the baker's last bun,
so I had to run.

He started to feel hot
in that really sunny spot
but he wanted the bun a lot
and would try until he got.

He really felt quite sick
as the bun he tried to nick
was about to get a lick
as the door started to click.

He opened up the door
and crawled across the floor
he wanted it more and more
but was shaken to the core.

I lick on my bun
that was such fun
better in my tum
yum, yum, yum.

Laura Burn (9)
St Fidelis Catholic School, Erith

My Animal Poem

One is the shark that had a heart
Two is the horse that took part
Three is the lizard that went green
Four is the cow that did lean
Five is the parrot that bit its tail
Six is the cat that ate a snail
Seven is the crock that ate a saw
Eight is a pig that broke the law
Nine is the bat that wanted to cook
Ten is the owl that read a book
Eleven is the bug that took part
Twelve is the tortoise that had a complaint
Thirteen is the rat that had a bat
Fourteen is the gorilla that was fat
Fifteen is the mouse that had a kiss
Sixteen is the elephant that did miss
Seventeen is the pup that did a dance
Eighteen is the cheetah that went to France
Nineteen is the giraffe that went to sea
Twenty is the foal that hurt its knee.

Sophie Price (7)
Staunton & Corse School, Gloucester

My Animal Poem

One is the horse that sat on a pin
Two is the slug that cut his chin
Three is the dog that bit his paw
Four is the cat that had kittens galore
Five is a fish that bit his tail
Six is the lion that sat on a slimy snail
Seven is the tiger that ate a man
Eight is the leopard that drove a van
Nine is the skunk that smelt bad
Ten is the pig that went mad.

Jack Collins (8)
Staunton & Corse School, Gloucester

My Animal Poem

One is the cat that slept on a bale
Two is the dog that bit his tail
Three is the horse that jumped a fence
Four is the slug that saved one pence
Five is the pig that ate some chalk
Six is a snake that ate some pork
Seven is the owl that read a book
Eight is the bird that wanted to cook
Nine is the rabbit that jumped a mile
Ten is the donkey that slept on a pile.

Isobel Caine (7)
Staunton & Corse School, Gloucester

The Crab

Red, scary crab pinches little crab
Snap, snap, snap, snap.
Don't pinch me, pinch your prey, pinch your prey
Snap, snap, snap, snap
Scaly crab scuttles to the rock pool, big and angry,
Snap, snap, snap, snap.

Laurie Cam (7)
Staunton & Corse School, Gloucester

Crab

Hot, angry, red
Crab swimming
Snap, snap, snap
Purple, calm crab
Snap, snap, snap
Orange, happy crab
The crab is going to bed

Dino Bradford (7)
Staunton & Corse School, Gloucester

My Ice Cream

Creamy, milky, icy ice cream, cooling me down
Soft pistachio tickling my tongue
Flake in cookie dough, *yum-yum,* icy ice cream.
Lick, lick, lick, Neapolitan, strawberry, vanilla and chocolate.
Scrunch, scrunch, yum-yum, icy ice cream
Orange pieces in my cool, cold ice cream,
Yum-yum, icy ice cream
Banana flavour milky cream
Double ice cream, toffee ripple and raspberry ripple.
Mint choc chip, *mmm yum*, my favourite.
Lovely!

Abigail Ball (7)
Staunton & Corse School, Gloucester

My Animal Poem

One is the shark that bit a horse
Two is the woodlouse that ate some sauce
Three is the lion that ate a rock
Four is the bird that laid a block
Five is the tiger that made a house
Six is the man that had a mouse.

Max Rayner (7)
Staunton & Corse School, Gloucester

My Animal Poem

One is the snail that lost the race
Two is the cat who entered the chase
Three is the cheetah that ran into a tree
Four is the giraffe that fell in the sea.

Rowan Smith (6)
Staunton & Corse School, Gloucester

My Animal Poem

One is the worm that cleaned the soil
Two is the dog that messed up the foil
Three is the bear that picked up a snail
Four is the pig that got a bit pale
Five is the chicken that got home in time
Six is the cow that ate all the lime
Seven is a tortoise that went very slow
Eight is the cat that caught a crow
Nine is the shark that got in a cuddle
Ten is the octopus that got in a muddle.

Matthew Cox (8)
Staunton & Corse School, Gloucester

My Animal Poem

One is the cat who sat on a mat
Two is the dog who ate the cat
Three is the chimpanzee who was in a tree
Four is a horse who ate a flea
Five is an owl who ate a snail
Six is a snake who ate away all!
Seven is a tiger who drank lots of cider.

Samuel Lane (7)
Staunton & Corse School, Gloucester

The Waves

Little blue waves are nice and kind,
Splash, Splash,
Medium waves helped me to swim
And are fun to jump in.
Big waves are fun when they lift me up,
And pull me down,
And are *angry*.

Chloe Cullen (8)
Staunton & Corse School, Gloucester

Fairy Tales

F airy tales fly away
A s if I've ever caught one.
I wish I could.
R eading on with temptation,
Y ou enter magical lands far away.

T he authors make it sound so real
A nd fill it all with joy.
L ooking at each word
E njoying the description
S o read fairy tales all day long!

Kate Morrison (8)
Westlea Primary School, Swindon

I Am . . .

I'm as
loud as a disco,
as quiet as a clam.

I'm as
messy as a dog,
neat as my work.

I'm as
shy as a mouse,
chatty as a chimp.

I'm as
brave as a lion,
frightened as a bunny.

I'm as
strange as a dream,
mysterious as an alien.

Beth Adams (7)
Westlea Primary School, Swindon

Seasons

Autumn reminds me of golden leaves
Swaying in the gentle breeze.

Winter reminds me of snowmen to make
And elegant and dainty snowflakes.

Spring reminds me of blooming flowers
But at this time the wind has no power.

Summer reminds me of sizzling heat
And the sun shining down on the bare grey street.

Seasons, seasons, what would England be without them?

Sophie Peart (9)
Westlea Primary School, Swindon

World War II

Bombs are exploding everywhere,
You can smell the poison in the air
And aeroplanes flying overhead,
Little children going to bed.

People screaming, people crying,
You can see the people dying.

Children getting on the train,
Saying bye to their mums in the pouring rain,
As the train doors shut,
The children get given one tiny nut.

People screaming, people crying,
You can see the people dying.

The war has ended,
Five years long,
And all the people sing a song.

Marcus Bateman (10)
Westlea Primary School, Swindon

Night

I curl up in my bed, petrified, anxious.
Will darkness really come tonight?
I remember it swooping in,
Scattering gloom all around me.

I hear a creak of the windows slowly opening
And *thump!* In comes this creature I have been dreading.
A robe is wrapped around it
I can't tell if it's a he or she
All I know is that it's arrived for me.

The creature roams toward me
As if it's trudging in treacle
I realise my mother has turned on the light
And that's the last time
I have seen night.

Faye Rogers (10)
Westlea Primary School, Swindon

Banana Sundae

As I tuck into my banana sundae,
I taste the yellow creamy banana bun,

I sit there still, yet I get a bit hot,
But I realise it's the burning feel of the sun,

I scream and shout and run straight home,
I run to my mum and tell her everything,

She tells me that I will be fine,
All I have to do is sing,

So I sing my favourite song,
I find myself in a distant land,

I look around and all I see,
Is sand scattered all over the floor.

Anna Waddington (10)
Westlea Primary School, Swindon

The Hobby

The hobby is floating like a kite over the trees.
It is going in no direction, just following the breeze.
Call as sharp and harsh as ice,
Gliding and diving further away,
I really wish it would stay.
It's going out of sight,
Back to its nest for the night.

Tess Pringle (9)
Westlea Primary School, Swindon

The Writer Of This Poem

(Based on 'The Writer of this Poem' by Roger McGough)

The writer of this poem
Is as complex as a puzzle
As creative as an artist
As soft as a teddy bear

As strong as a wrestling champ
As smart as a scientist
As polite as a waiter
As refreshing as ice

As quick as a cheetah
As talented as a stage performer
As shy as a mouse
As daft as a clown

The writer of this poem
Is as deep as the ocean
He has a heart of gold
(or so the poem says).

Jack Adams (10)
Westlea Primary School, Swindon